5 STEPS TO A

5™

500

AP U.S. Government and Politics Questions
to know by test day

D0823900

5 STEPS TO A >5™

500

AP U.S. Government and Politics Questions

to know by test day

William Madden

Brian T. Stevens

New York Chicago San Francisco Athens London Madrid Mexico City
Milan New Delhi Singapore Sydney Toronto

WILLIAM MADDEN is a history teacher who has taught AP classes in U.S. government and comparative government for the last several years. Prior to becoming a history teacher, he was a senior account executive for a health care public relations agency in New York City, where he became familiar with government regulation and the media. A graduate of Rutgers University, he holds degrees in political science and English.

BRIAN T. STEVENS is a AP reader and table leader, College Board consultant, AP book editor and U.S. government and politics instructor who has taught AP U.S. Government & Politics instructor for the past 27 years. Over the course of those years Brian has had hundreds of his students pass the AP test, most years beating the national passing average by 25 or more percentage points. A graduate of Western Michigan University and Michigan State University, he holds degrees in political science and U.S. constitutional history.

1 2 3 4 5 6 7 8 9   QFR   23 22 21 20 19 18

ISBN   978-1-259-83648-0
MHID   1-259-83648-7

e-ISBN   978-1-259-83649-7
e-MHID   1-259-83649-5

Series interior design by Jane Tennenbaum.

McGraw-Hill Education books are available at special quantity discounts to use as premiums and sales promotions, or for use in corporate training programs. To contact a representative, please visit the Contact Us pages at www.mhprofessional.com.

CONTENTS

INTRODUCTION

Congratulations! You've taken a big step toward AP success by purchasing *5 Steps to a 5: 500 AP U.S. Government and Politics Questions to Know by Test Day.* We are here to help you take the next step and score high on your AP exam so you can earn college credits and get into the college or university of your choice.

This book gives you 500 AP-style multiple-choice questions that cover all the most essential course material. Each question has a detailed explanation with the answer. These questions will give you valuable independent practice to supplement your regular textbook and the groundwork you are already doing in your AP classroom. This and the other books in this series were written by expert AP teachers who know your exam inside out and can identify the crucial information you will need to know as well as questions that are most likely to appear on the exam.

You may be the kind of student who takes several AP courses and needs to study extra questions a few weeks before the exam for a final review. Or you may be the kind who puts off preparing until the last weeks before the exam. No matter what your preparation style is, you will surely benefit from reviewing these 500 questions, which closely parallel the content, format, and degree of difficulty of those on the actual AP exam. These questions and their answers/explanations are the ideal last-minute study tool for those final few weeks before the test.

Remember the old saying "Practice makes perfect." If you practice with all the questions and answers in this book, we are certain you will build the skills and confidence you will need to do great on the exam. Good luck!

—Editors of McGraw-Hill Education

PREFACE

Welcome to the revised edition of *5 Steps To A 5: 500 AP U.S. Government and Politics Questions*. This edition reflects the changes you will find in the newly redesigned 2018-2019 AP test. There will now be four answers on multiple-choice questions instead of five, and questions will be organized by the new curriculum framework aptly named the Big Ideas. The redesigned AP test will also feature many questions on Supreme Court cases, including a focus on the 15 landmark cases mandated for the new test. This edition also includes a detailed answer explanation for each question in order to help you do your best on test day.

Best of luck!

PART 1

Foundations of American Democracy

CHAPTER 1

Constitutional Foundations

1. The Constitutional Convention sought to replace the Articles of Confederation because they
    (A) created a large central government
    (B) guaranteed a separation of powers
    (C) failed to provide for states' rights
    (D) did not have the ability to tax and provide for the common defense

2. This was the policy of the British government toward the colonies after the French and Indian War that sowed the seeds of revolution.
    (A) Salutary neglect
    (B) Navigation Acts
    (C) Royal charters
    (D) Stamp Act

3. A pivotal event that symbolized the problems with the Articles of Confederation and demonstrated the need to reform the Articles was
    (A) Shays's Rebellion
    (B) Nat Turner's Rebellion
    (C) the failure of all states to send troops for defense against a new British attack
    (D) a national tax to help pay the debt incurred by the Revolutionary War

4. During the Articles of Confederation problems persisted because all of the following EXCEPT
    (A) The United States was not a major exporter of goods.
    (B) Congress could pass laws with 9 out 13 states.
    (C) The executive branch was weak.
    (D) The national government was incapable of responding to other nations' trade sanctions against the United States.

5. Popular uprisings in states such as Massachusetts, Virginia, and Pennsylvania led state legislatures to overturn unpopular court decisions and to

   (A) arrest tax collectors and judges
   (B) appeal for economic relief from the national government
   (C) station a standing militia in particular places of unrest
   (D) alter property assessments and issue devalued money

6. The Constitution creates a system that prevents excessive power being accumulated by the national government through

   (A) judicial review
   (B) federalism
   (C) checks and balances
   (D) representative government

7. According to Alexander Hamilton, a strong central government was required for the United States to compete with the rest of the world on a(n) _____ level.

   (A) economic
   (B) political
   (C) military
   (D) All of the above

8. The Anti-Federalists' opposition to the Constitution was predicated on the belief that a strong central government would

   (A) empower the general public and undermine government officials
   (B) create states that were free to act in their own interests
   (C) not be an effective way to deal with other nations
   (D) strip states and individuals of their rights and the authority to make laws

9. The Federalist Papers—a series of essays by Alexander Hamilton, James Madison, and John Jay—were originally meant to assist which state to ratify the Constitution?

   (A) New York
   (B) New Jersey
   (C) Massachusetts
   (D) Pennsylvania

10. The Constitution differs from the Declaration of Independence in that it does not focus on the individual rights of the governed, but rather on
    - (A) the rights of the government
    - (B) the synthesis of government and citizen
    - (C) the structure and function of the government
    - (D) the promotion of a republican system

11. The primary economic failure of the Articles of Confederation was that
    - (A) national debt needed to be paid off by individual states
    - (B) Congress could not collect taxes
    - (C) there was no system for states to pay back their debts
    - (D) individuals were taxed directly by the national government

12. The commerce clause expands Congress's power, because it gives the national legislature the authority to
    - (A) collect taxes from individual citizens
    - (B) collect taxes from private businesses
    - (C) nationalize certain legislative policy
    - (D) supersede state law

13. The constitutional provision that allows Congress to expand its legislative power is the
    - (A) supremacy clause
    - (B) necessary and proper clause
    - (C) commerce clause
    - (D) implied powers clause

14. Historically, the most frequent method for amending the Constitution has been for
    - (A) two-thirds of the states to request a constitutional convention to ratify a new amendment
    - (B) a two-thirds vote in Congress to be followed by ratification in three-fourths of the state legislatures
    - (C) three-fourths of special state constitutional conventions to ratify a new amendment
    - (D) a three-fourths vote in Congress to be followed by ratification in two-thirds of the state legislatures

15. The importance of the separation of powers in the American government system is
    (A) protection of citizens from government intrusion
    (B) limitations of the federal government's power
    (C) clearly defined responsibilities and authority for each branch
    (D) executive authority that ensures the other branches meet their responsibilities

16. All tax legislation must begin with
    (A) the Senate
    (B) the President
    (C) the states
    (D) the House of Representatives

17. The plan proposed by James Madison at the Constitutional Convention that was the foundation of the structure of Congress was the
    (A) New Jersey Plan
    (B) Connecticut Plan
    (C) Virginia Plan
    (D) Great Compromise

18. The New Jersey Plan, an alternative to the Virginia Plan, received states' rights support because it
    (A) created an independent judiciary
    (B) created a powerful executive
    (C) maintained representation based on the population of a state
    (D) maintained the one state–one vote structure that existed under the Articles of Confederation

19. The Constitution grants Congress explicit powers in
    (A) Article I, Section 3
    (B) Article I, Section 8
    (C) Article I, Section 7
    (D) Article I, Section 5

20. The Seventeenth Amendment altered the original structure of dual federalism toward shared federalism by
    (A) allowing the direct election of senators
    (B) creating a national income tax
    (C) allowing the federal government to prevent the sale of alcohol
    (D) providing due process to state law

21. In the case Marbury v. Madison the Supreme Court established the Court's ability to

(A) Practice judicial restraint
(B) Declare laws unconstitutional
(C) Exercise its appellate jurisdiction
(D) Utilize judicial activism

CHAPTER 2

Federalism, Checks and Balances, & Separation of Powers

22. According to the Constitution local governments receive power from
    - (A) Article IV
    - (B) Article VI
    - (C) Amendment 9
    - (D) Amendment 10

23. Which of the following is a key component of federalism?
    - (A) Each level of government is independent from other levels.
    - (B) The national government supersedes other, lower levels.
    - (C) Lower levels of government do not exert political leverage on higher levels.
    - (D) Federalism allows for self-governance at the local level.

24. Federalism is a hybrid arrangement of two forms of government called
    - (A) parliamentary and republican
    - (B) parliamentary and unitary
    - (C) confederation and unitary
    - (D) confederation and democracy

25. All of the following are constitutional provisions for federalism EXCEPT
    - (A) Article IV, Section 3
    - (B) The Twelfth Amendment
    - (C) The Tenth Amendment
    - (D) Article VI

26. Federal laws that allow states to administer joint federal-state programs are
    - (A) partial preemptions
    - (B) crossover sanctions
    - (C) federal mandates
    - (D) crosscutting requirements

27. In 1962 the Supreme Court declared that legislative districts must be designed to be roughly equal in size with this case
    (A) Baker v. Carr
    (B) Wesberry v. Sanders
    (C) Citizens United v. FEC
    (D) Shelby County v. Holder

28. Unfunded mandates pose a significant burden to states because
    (A) federal policies are attached to mandates that states may have to fund entirely
    (B) states are forced to administer policies to which they might object
    (C) they reduce state authority
    (D) All of the above

29. Under the federal system, the type of federal grant-in-aid that causes states to spend less carefully is the
    (A) block grant
    (B) matching grant
    (C) categorical grant
    (D) grants-in-aid

30. Through the power of the purse, the federal government uses this to control the actions of the states
    (A) categorical grants
    (B) block grants
    (C) funded mandates
    (D) All of the above

31. Competitive federalism is the idea that
    (A) states maneuver for favored position with the national government
    (B) the national government grants more aid to states that are willing to cede control
    (C) states can experiment with reform and, if successful, their methods can be replicated elsewhere
    (D) the national government grants more to states that perform better

32. Lyndon B. Johnson's War on Poverty, part of his Great Society, shifted federalism toward nationalism by
    (A) funding state programs through federal grants
    (B) taking over the operation of schools in urban districts
    (C) creating jobs for those living below the poverty line
    (D) forcing states to provide housing for the poor

33. Franklin D. Roosevelt's New Deal shifted federalism toward nationalism by

(A) superseding state authority
(B) providing money to bankrupt states
(C) funding state-run banks
(D) regulating and financing state action

34. Stipulations of government funding that requires states to adhere to specific guidelines are called:

(A) Mandates
(B) Conditions of Aid
(C) Judicial edicts
(D) Grants in Aid

35. The amendment that applies the rights guaranteed in the Bill of Rights to state law is the

(A) Thirteenth
(B) Fourteenth
(C) Fifteenth
(D) Sixteenth

36. What Supreme Court case began to establish the extended reach of federal authority?

(A) *Marbury v. Madison*
(B) *Gibbons v. Ogden*
(C) *McCulloch v. Maryland*
(D) *Gitlow v. New York*

37. How has the supremacy clause allowed for ever-greater national authority?

(A) National law automatically supersedes state law.
(B) States are forced to react to national government action or legislation.
(C) Congress is the only legislative body that can increase its authority.
(D) The national government is in charge of all taxation.

38. Under the federal system, which type of federal grant-in-aid gives states an exact amount to spend?

(A) Categorical grants
(B) Matching grants
(C) Treasury grants
(D) Block grants

39. James Madison, as stated in Federalist No. 10, believed that _____ could lead to a "tyranny of the majority."
    (A) corrupt officials
    (B) larger states abusing smaller states
    (C) factions
    (D) regional differences between the North and South

40. John Locke, an Enlightenment philosopher, influenced American constitutional theory with his
    (A) Advocacy of separation of powers
    (B) Inventing the concept of federalism
    (C) Social contract theory
    (D) Legislative supremacy

41. Thomas Jefferson's version of the Declaration of the Independence was largely impacted by the writings of
    (A) Montesquieu
    (B) Hume
    (C) Rosseuau
    (D) Locke

42. John Locke and Montesquieu both championed _____ in their political philosophy.
    (A) governmental control
    (B) equal representation in government
    (C) authoritarian government
    (D) limited government

43. The inherent structure of the Constitution that allows U.S. citizens to delegate who has authority and allows that authority to be removed is most attributable to which political philosopher?
    (A) John Locke
    (B) Thomas Hobbes
    (C) David Hume
    (D) Montesquieu

44. Montesquieu promoted the idea of separation of powers through the adoption of

(A) a strong executive
(B) representative government
(C) political parties
(D) an independent judiciary

45. The social contract theory calls for an agreement between

(A) The people and the government
(B) The national government and state governments
(C) State and local governments
(D) The people and God

46. According to James Madison, the republican form of government addresses the tyranny of the majority through

(A) factionalization
(B) pluralism
(C) limited government
(D) democratization

47. States are authorized to redraw congressional districts following each U.S. Census and often create districts favorable to the party in power in a process called

(A) realignment
(B) gerrymandering
(C) reapportionment
(D) logrolling

48. Constitutionally, the president does not have much legislative authority because

(A) foreign affairs are more of a concern
(B) the Founding Fathers placed the executive at the end of the legislative process
(C) Article II of the Constitution is not clear on the president's enumerated powers
(D) the president defers to Congress on policy

49. The presidential veto is referred to as an exclusively negative construct because it
    (A) blocks congressional legislation
    (B) alters legislative packages while they are being created
    (C) does not allow the president to propose alternative legislation
    (D) All of the above

50. The creation of the federal bureaucracy is due to the constitutional management of
    (A) Congress creating executive branches
    (B) the president delegating executive authority
    (C) the judiciary interpreting laws
    (D) the states retaining the same authority as the federal government

51. Constitutional courts, whether the Supreme Court or lower-level courts, derive their authority from _____ of the Constitution.
    (A) Article I
    (B) Article II
    (C) Article III
    (D) Article IV

52. Federal courts have limited jurisdiction, which means
    (A) they can hear only cases regarding the national government
    (B) they can hear only cases concerning federal questions and citizens of different states
    (C) they cannot hear cases in which Congress is involved
    (D) they cannot hear cases involving charges against the president

53. The Supreme Court maintains its position of authority over lower federal courts through
    (A) how well it communicates its decisions
    (B) the remanding of cases down to the lower courts
    (C) an ability to decide what cases are heard
    (D) its ability to overturn lower-court decisions

54. All of the following are limits the Supreme Court can place over the federal judiciary EXCEPT
    (A) Life tenure insulates judges from each other.
    (B) The Supreme Court cannot easily force the implementation of decisions.
    (C) It is difficult for the Supreme Court to remove lower-court judges.
    (D) The cost of continually monitoring lower courts is prohibitive.

55. A writ of certiorari is

(A) the official denial from the Supreme Court to hear a case
(B) the official request to hear a lower-court case
(C) the official acceptance from the Supreme Court to hear a case
(D) the official order to a lower court to reverse a decision

56. Amicus curiae briefs and solicitor general support may often lead the Supreme Court to grant certiorari because

(A) the solicitor general is the lead attorney for the U.S. government
(B) both amicus briefs and the solicitor general set the agenda for the court
(C) amicus briefs and the solicitor general indirectly let the court know which cases are most significant
(D) amicus briefs and the solicitor general are part of most cases appealed to the court

57. Stare decisis, or "let the decision stand," is an example of _____ doctrine.

(A) substantive
(B) judicial
(C) procedural
(D) traditional

58. The departmental theory of constitutional review holds that

(A) the judiciary is the sole arbiter of the activities of all three branches
(B) each branch checks the other two
(C) the checks and balances system is limited by each branch
(D) the executive and legislative branches can interpret the separation of powers

59. The Founding Fathers did not agree with political parties or factions because of such entities'

(A) disorganized nature
(B) undermining of the authority of elected representatives
(C) natural tendency toward discord rather than reconciliation
(D) dangerous influence on good government

60. State and local governments are typically at odds with the national government over
    (A) mandates
    (B) funding
    (C) states' rights
    (D) representation

61. A major debate the states have with the national government over federalism is
    (A) the practice that allows a policy in one state (that harms no other state) to be changed by the national government
    (B) federal funding
    (C) their dependency on the national government
    (D) the burden of the federal bureaucracy

62. The states' primary recourse for arguing against national law is through
    (A) appealing to the federal judiciary
    (B) appealing to the executive branch
    (C) altering the federal bureaucracy
    (D) appealing directly to the people

63. State prerogatives in national government considerations began to wane with
    (A) the establishment of the income tax
    (B) the rise in power of the president
    (C) the national programs of the New Deal
    (D) the direct election of senators

64. Originally, the supremacy clause of the Constitution was meant only to
    (A) bring states into the national fold
    (B) interpret what state legislation was constitutional
    (C) avoid impasses over jurisdiction
    (D) cede authority to the national government

65. The Tenth Amendment offers the most explicit endorsement of federalism, because it
    (A) states that all powers not given to the national government rest with state governments
    (B) states that all powers not given to the national government rest with the people
    (C) provides for a clear separation between national and state governments
    (D) establishes the spheres of influence of each level of government

66. The Tenth Amendment has not been effective in defending states' rights due to the supremacy clause and what other constitutional clause?
    (A) Commerce
    (B) Elastic
    (C) Take care
    (D) Due process

67. The erosion of state government power in many areas is due to
    (A) increased spending by the national government
    (B) the national regulation of industry
    (C) the growth of the bureaucracy
    (D) public goods encompassing the larger, national community

68. Granting national authority to policies that affect only single states can lead to
    (A) a rational outcome
    (B) better-funded policy
    (C) heavy burdens on the state(s) in question
    (D) a disgruntled electorate

69. Federal-state relations have changed because Americans have sometimes decided to
    (A) adopt policies of such magnitude that no one state could handle them
    (B) side with the national government due to its resources
    (C) side with their state governments due to the proximity
    (D) vote new politicians into office

70. Federal intervention has also been warranted when
    (A) states have not been able to solve their problems by working together
    (B) states have refused to abide by federal laws
    (C) states have refused to abide by Supreme Court rulings
    (D) bureaucracies have taken over government programs

71. States have given up control to federal authority because
    (A) they have been forced to by Congress
    (B) an executive order was issued
    (C) the public demanded it
    (D) it was easier on their internal government structures

72. The innovation of the New Deal in regard to federalism was with
    (A) its policies
    (B) Roosevelt's vocal championing of its policies
    (C) its size and scope
    (D) the permanent change in the regulatory structure

73. State government power may continue to diminish in some areas due to
    (A) funding requirements
    (B) the increased power of federal politicians
    (C) increased bureaucracy
    (D) the states' continued collective action dilemmas

74. The federal system occasionally encourages states to "race to the bottom" in social service because
    (A) funding cutbacks are economically helpful
    (B) states do not want to provide stellar public services so others move there and burden the system
    (C) the electorate rarely cares about social issues
    (D) states want more government funding

75. Although the federal courts are where states may seek a ruling in their favor,
    (A) the judiciary often sides with the national government
    (B) the Supreme Court usually finds for the national government
    (C) economic issues almost always move toward national control
    (D) states are often forced to comply with government regulations

76. State governments have an advantage in that
    (A) they are more connected to their constituents
    (B) public opinion has moved away from supporting the federal government
    (C) recent Supreme Court decisions do not automatically find for the federal government
    (D) their political parties are better organized than those on the national level

77. The federal-state relationship changed in the twentieth century due to
    (A) powerful political parties
    (B) an increase in the bureaucracy required
    (C) bursts of national policymaking
    (D) the increased power of the president

78. The president is not as involved with federal-state issues because

    (A) he or she is not directly elected by the people
    (B) he or she holds the only office in America that voted nationally
    (C) his or her focus is on the bureaucracy
    (D) All of the above

79. The greatest connection between the state and federal governments is through

    (A) political parties
    (B) mandates
    (C) public policy
    (D) government spending

80. One of the problems faced by states that has driven the federal government to nationalize many policies is

    (A) increases in population
    (B) technology
    (C) coordination
    (D) federal grants

81. National public policy reduces the possibility of the states engaging in behavior called

    (A) unconstitutional cooperation
    (B) cutthroat competition
    (C) disregard for other states
    (D) economic discrimination

82. The Supreme Court interprets and influences public policy and government action by

    (A) using the Constitution
    (B) correcting any practice it thinks is undemocratic
    (C) considering the legislative intent
    (D) using past precedents

83. Unlike the other branches of government and bureaucracy, the judiciary can change policy only if

    (A) it deems such changes necessary through judicial writ
    (B) a case is brought to its attention and is within its jurisdiction
    (C) the change is requested by one of the other branches
    (D) the change is requested by a majority of the states

84. *Bush v. Gore* demonstrated the importance of the Supreme Court by
    (A) having it settle perhaps the most contentious presidential race in modern American history
    (B) designating it the final arbiter of a decision that had broad political and policy implications
    (C) the fact that it was not damaged by its controversial and seemingly political decision
    (D) All of the above

85. The states are the fundamental building blocks of the federal system and are pivotal in creating policy because
    (A) state legislatures are important partners with the federal government
    (B) senators represent states at the national level
    (C) federal policy and programs are administered through the states
    (D) the structure of the Constitution grants states a level of policymaking authority

86. The structure of federalism forces effective policy to be made
    (A) at the executive level
    (B) at the national level
    (C) at the state level
    (D) at the legislative level

87. Regional and local conflicts over policy issues do not necessarily rise to national prominence because
    (A) public policy tends to remain local
    (B) the federal structure separates the national and state governments
    (C) the two-party system effectively suppresses regionalism
    (D) local leaders want to maintain their political power

88. The judicial interpretation method that says legislation must meet the intent of the wording of the Constitution and amendments is
    (A) loose scrutiny
    (B) judicial scrutiny
    (C) strict scrutiny
    (D) legislative scrutiny

89. Deferential scrutiny of legislation by the Supreme Court means that
    (A) Congress is given leeway in the intent of legislation
    (B) legislation doesn't have to match the wording of the Constitution perfectly
    (C) the intent of legislation is fully considered
    (D) All of the above

90. Judicial ideology is a benefit rather than a hindrance to democratic responsibility because
    (A) it allows the president and Congress to keep the judiciary from straying too far from majority opinion
    (B) it is consistent over time due to the life tenure of federal judges
    (C) it allows the other branches to have influence over judicial policy
    (D) All of the above

91. The Supreme Court is the branch of government that protects civil liberties because
    (A) it alone interprets the constitutionality of legislation
    (B) it was designed to avoid the passions of even vast majorities
    (C) it can define what civil liberties Americans enjoy
    (D) All of the above

92. The supremacy of the federal government over the states was firmly established in what case?
    (A) McCulloch v. Maryland
    (B) Marbury v. Madison
    (C) Barron v. Baltimore
    (D) Gibbons v. Ogden

93. The mutual vetoes in the separation of powers and checks and balances system ensures that generally
    (A) national and state power remain separate
    (B) state governments have some political power
    (C) politicians work for their constituents
    (D) the executive has a role in legislative policy

94. The judicial branch's primary power in the checks and balances system is
    (A) declaring laws and executive orders unconstitutional
    (B) overseeing impeachment trials for high-ranking government officials
    (C) having original jurisdiction over international treaties
    (D) overseeing the function of lower federal courts

95. As part of the checks and balances system, Congress has the power to

(A) nominate top executive appointments
(B) nominate all federal judges
(C) create international treaties
(D) confirm all federal judges

96. Our judicial system derives its power and authority from

(A) its independence from elective politics
(B) its influence on government policy
(C) its responsibility for interpreting laws
(D) its connection to the American public

PART 2

Interaction Among Branches of Government

CHAPTER 3

Congress and Policy Making

97. All of the following are reasons senators have a more difficult time getting reelected than their House counterparts EXCEPT

  (A) States tend to be more diverse than districts, and building a loyal constituency is more difficult.

  (B) Statewide elections have a more balanced competition between the major parties.

  (C) Senate races attract more talented, wealthier candidates to compete for the office.

  (D) The length of a Senate term provides challengers more information to make a case against a sitting senator.

98. Congressional committees and subcommittees exist

  (A) to acquire the information needed to pass meaningful and comprehensive legislation

  (B) to offer important political posts to influential representatives and senators

  (C) to consolidate power in the majority party

  (D) to streamline the ever-growing legislative process

99. In today's complex and busy Congress, party leaders' power is bolstered by their ability to

  (A) tell other party members how to vote

  (B) control messaging to the press

  (C) direct the flow of bills through the legislative process

  (D) distribute party contributions to those members most in need of financing

100. The rules and procedures of Congress are designed generally to

  (A) coordinate legislation

  (B) resolve conflicts

  (C) form constituencies

  (D) reduce the conformity costs to individual members

101. One of the largest legislative considerations for the House of Representatives is time, because
    (A) members need to campaign constantly to hold on to their offices
    (B) the media have a 24-hour news cycle
    (C) coordinating 435 members is often a difficult process
    (D) the House must pass a federal budget every year

102. Which committee in the House of Representatives is an instrument of the majority party?
    (A) Rules Committee
    (B) Conference Committee
    (C) Steering Committee
    (D) Ways and Means Committee

103. Who are the representatives in each party that form the communication network that bring each party together?
    (A) Majority leaders
    (B) Minority leaders
    (C) Committee chairs
    (D) Whips

104. The Senate is less formal than the House because coordination is not as difficult. The Senate organizes its business through
    (A) party agreements
    (B) a floor vote
    (C) filibuster
    (D) unanimous consent agreements

105. All of the following are types of committees in Congress EXCEPT
    (A) Select
    (B) Party
    (C) Standing
    (D) Conference

106. For a law to be passed, there are _____ steps between the introduction of a bill and sending it to the president's desk.
    (A) four
    (B) two
    (C) six
    (D) seven

107. Congress usually maintains the status quo regarding legislation because

(A) it is far easier to kill a bill than to pass one
(B) several coalitions have to be made to pass legislation
(C) that was the Founding Fathers' intent
(D) All of the above

108. The current budgetary woes of the federal government stem from entitlement legislation that

(A) automatically divides up the yearly federal budget
(B) designates specific classes of people who are entitled to a legally defined benefit
(C) separates the House and Senate and prevents them from working together on certain issues
(D) is designed to prevent legislation from passing quickly and being sent to the president without hearings and debate

109. What congressional institution audits and reports on programs and agencies?

(A) Inspectors general
(B) Specific subcommittees
(C) The Office of Mandatory Reports
(D) The Government Accountability Office (GAO)

110. Hearings and investigations are important for bureaucracies because they

(A) help explain and defend positions
(B) establish relationships with key members of Congress
(C) provide an opportunity to request more congressional support
(D) allow bureaucrats to question congressional leaders

111. All of the following are reasons that Congress might delegate authority to other branches or bureaucracies EXCEPT

(A) It needs time to fulfill all of its responsibilities.
(B) It lacks the expertise.
(C) The Constitution requires it.
(D) It needs to remain flexible.

112. The War Powers Act actually may have given the president more ability to wage war because

    (A) it ignores the constitutional responsibility of the legislature
    (B) it ignores the constitutional responsibility of the executive
    (C) it lessens the restrictions on presidential authority
    (D) it implies that the president can wage war without congressional approval

113. Which of the following is a significant tactic Congress can use to maintain the balance of power with the executive and judicial branches and bureaucracies?

    (A) Holding investigations
    (B) Passing laws
    (C) Taking ideological stands on issues
    (D) Taking positions on issues that usually fall to one of the other groups

114. In addition to getting reelected, members of Congress have an incentive to influence bureaucracies by

    (A) addressing policy concerns that ensure Congress gets what it wants
    (B) keeping power away from the executive branch to ensure control over policy
    (C) giving responsibility to the executive branch to share the responsibility
    (D) keeping interest groups happy to ease changes in policy

115. Legislative vetoes were found unconstitutional in theory because

    (A) they undermined the intent of the Constitution
    (B) they placed federal bureaucracies under congressional control
    (C) they were temporary solutions to executive problems
    (D) they undermined the judiciary

116. A legislative veto is

    (A) an agreement between the executive and legislative branches
    (B) an instance of Congress ignoring a Supreme Court ruling
    (C) an instance of Congress overriding an executive policy
    (D) a law that overrides an existing law

117. Which of the following cases represents an instance where Congress did not follow a Supreme Court decision, demonstrating the court's lack of authority in enforcing its decisions?

   (A) *Kelo v. City of New London*
   (B) *Immigration and Naturalization Service v. Chadha*
   (C) *Hamdi v. Rumsfeld*
   (D) *Rasul v. Bush*

118. The most important factor influencing whether a member of Congress can affect agency action is whether he or she is

   (A) a member of the majority party
   (B) a representative of a constituency affected by a particular agency action
   (C) a member of a committee with jurisdiction over the agency
   (D) affiliated with certain interest groups

119. The primary beneficiaries of detailed statutory instructions are

   (A) the agency being instructed
   (B) those served by the agency
   (C) employees of the agency
   (D) congressional committee members

120. When party control in Congress is powerful, rather than committees of individuals, the relationship between Congress and the bureaucracy relies on

   (A) detailed statutes
   (B) expert testimony at hearings
   (C) investigations of certain uncooperative agencies
   (D) budgetary tools and appropriation bills

121. All of the following are methods that members of Congress can use to influence agency action EXCEPT

   (A) budgetary controls
   (B) statutory instructions
   (C) oversight
   (D) legislative veto

122. Senators have more influence in policymaking than House members because

    (A) most federal domestic-assistance funds go to state governments
    (B) senators serve longer terms
    (C) senators are better known to the public
    (D) there is a large difference in size between the two chambers of Congress

123. Most bills that reach the floor for debate in Congress are not controversial because

    (A) they represent the clear preferences of the American people
    (B) the party in control handles the wording of most of the bills
    (C) the committee system allows for the avoidance of controversial legislation
    (D) many bills involve the renewal or revision of existing programs and previous legislation

124. Congressional committees allow politicians to pursue all three activities that help reelection bids: advertising, credit claiming, and

    (A) position taking
    (B) public policy formation
    (C) oversight
    (D) media exposure

125. Taking clear positions on committees allows politicians to

    (A) control bureaucracies
    (B) keep the executive branch in check
    (C) create legislation that will pass judicial muster
    (D) associate themselves with popular policy or distance themselves from unpopular policy

126. In an era of partisan politics, policy views become homogeneous, so committees are used to

    (A) clarify policy
    (B) establish greater party and legislative influence
    (C) temper executive action through investigations
    (D) harness public opinion

127. Reducing the size of congressional committees is difficult to accomplish because

    (A) there is less chance for officials to claim credit for successful programs

    (B) the primary goal for politicians on committees is to deliver benefits to their constituencies

    (C) it threatens the unity of the party in power

    (D) All of the above

128. Committee representation reflecting the membership depends on

    (A) the party in power

    (B) the party leadership's control of the committee process

    (C) the reach of the committee

    (D) the issues the committee considers

129. House leadership has more control over committee output than the Senate due to the

    (A) standing committees

    (B) subcommittees

    (C) Rules Committee

    (D) Ways and Means Committee

130. The method that has allowed Congress to adjust bureaucratic action and procedural rules is

    (A) issuing a federal waiver

    (B) turning authority over to the executive branch

    (C) taking back control from federal agencies

    (D) altering the responsibilities of federal agencies

131. Senators are more influential in policy formation than their House counterparts because

    (A) they have more control of the bureaucracy

    (B) individual members are more important due to the different sizes of the Senate and House

    (C) they tend to have more expertise on policy issues

    (D) they are more closely connected to their constituents

132. The current difficulties in the committee system stem from

    (A) electoral politics and party competition

    (B) the nature and structure of committees

    (C) the shifting landscape of public opinion

    (D) parochialism

CHAPTER 4

The Presidency, Bureaucracy and Policy Making

133. When the President uses his/her stature through the media to promote their policy then he/she is using the:

(A) Bully Pulpit

(B) Power of the purse

(C) Ability to take over the media through executive orders

(D) Role of Commander in Chief

134. In the nineteenth century, presidents gave close attention to their cabinet nominees because

(A) during the days of party dominance, such nominees represented important interests within the party

(B) cabinets played important supportive roles to a powerful executive

(C) they needed individuals who would be competent

(D) cabinet members were loyal to the president

135. Prior to electoral reforms, the presidency was the focal point of party politics for all of the following reasons EXCEPT

(A) As a method of control of federal patronage positions

(B) The president was in control of the legislative agenda.

(C) If a party carried the presidency, it carried congressional elections as well.

(D) The president was the figurehead of the party in power nationally and usually regionally.

136. As commander in chief of the armed forces, the president has the power to

(A) declare war

(B) hold the highest rank in the military

(C) ratify peace treaties

(D) None of the above

137. As chief diplomat, the president can use _____ as a means of avoiding the treaty ratification process in Congress.

(A) executive agreements
(B) signing statements
(C) recognition of the legitimacy of countries
(D) presidential summits with other leaders

138. The president's right to withhold information from Congress is

(A) national security privilege
(B) executive privilege
(C) presidential privilege
(D) executive prerogative

139. Executive orders are

(A) responsibilities delegated by the president
(B) responsibilities delegated to the president
(C) formal instructions issued to the president
(D) formal instructions issued by the president

140. Presidents have authority to issue executive orders because of

(A) Reserved powers
(B) Delegated powers
(C) Inherent powers
(D) Concurrent powers

141. Presidential influence and leadership have tracked with the growth of the national government because

(A) the media allow presidents to communicate more effectively
(B) stronger, more qualified candidates have become willing to run
(C) the public has begun to participate more in elections and politics
(D) Congress has delegated more administrative tasks to the president

142. One of the most important ways modern presidents are able to impact the direction of government is through

(A) the annual budget
(B) the take care clause
(C) their role as commander in chief
(D) the bully pulpit

143. One explicit constitutional responsibility given to the president that has enabled modern presidents to mobilize public opinion is

    (A) the Office of Management and Budget (OMB)
    (B) the State of the Union address
    (C) executive orders
    (D) being commander in chief

144. The OMB is a vital part of the Executive Office of the President (EOP) because it oversees

    (A) military activities outside of those overseen by the Pentagon
    (B) central clearance
    (C) congressional committees
    (D) the White House staff

145. In the nineteenth century, the rotation in office and the spoils system led to the bureaucratization of government workers, because

    (A) individuals made careers out of government jobs
    (B) these systems were the primary sources for maintaining party machines
    (C) these systems allowed many qualified applicants to get government jobs
    (D) the executive branch had oversight instead of Congress

146. The primary level of federal bureaucracy that helps the president and Congress administer policy is

    (A) congressional committees
    (B) the Executive Office of the President
    (C) the cabinet
    (D) the Office of Management and Budget (OMB)

147. The departments of Agriculture, Labor, and Commerce differ from the Treasury, the Justice Department, and the Department of Defense because the former

    (A) serve general social purposes
    (B) do not represent a particular clientele
    (C) naturally grew out of the needs of society
    (D) do not need anyone to lobby on their behalf

148. Which Cabinet department employs the most people?

    (A) State Department

    (B) Defense Department

    (C) Interior Department

    (D) Department of Labor

149. All of the following cabinet departments were created in response to social need and an extension of federal authority EXCEPT

    (A) the Department of Health and Human Services

    (B) the Department of Housing and Urban Development

    (C) the Department of Veterans Affairs

    (D) the Department of Energy

150. What Cabinet department was created as a reaction to the September 11, 2001 terrorist attacks?

    (A) Homeland Security

    (B) Defense Department

    (C) State Department

    (D) National Security Agency

151. Bureaucratic agencies that are placed outside of cabinet departments to achieve political goals for the president are

    (A) government corporations

    (B) regulatory commissions

    (C) executive agencies

    (D) subcabinet departments

152. Regulatory commissions are bureaucratic agencies that

    (A) maintain their independence from the president and executive departments

    (B) allow the president to control the administration of certain programs

    (C) prevent Congress from utilizing party politics to achieve political goals

    (D) allow Congress to regulate certain industries directly

153. Government corporations are created by Congress to

    (A) offer specific services

    (B) act as private companies would

    (C) rehabilitate an industry that has lost market support

    (D) All of the above

154. Indirect administration is a way for federal bureaucracies to operate programs

 (A) but incur costs from private contractors
 (B) but reduce the federal bureaucracy
 (C) but at a political cost to officeholders
 (D) but deny private companies access to the programs

155. Bureaucrats suffer all of the following EXCEPT

 (A) the hyperpolitical nature of their jobs
 (B) a lack of institutional autonomy
 (C) infighting between agencies and departments
 (D) distribution problems of their services

156. The president has control of executive bureaucracies; this control is exercised best through

 (A) the veto power
 (B) the power of appointment
 (C) the confirmation of the cabinet
 (D) the oversight of the bureaucracies

157. The War Powers Act of 1973 sought to

 (A) remove the president's ability to declare war
 (B) create a committee to determine whether American military involvement was necessary
 (C) end the Vietnam War
 (D) require the president to notify Congress within 48 hours of committing troops

158. Presidents do not issue orders to bureaucracies to get them to comply with his or her agenda because

 (A) manipulation through organized interest groups works better
 (B) presidents do not have total authority
 (C) the bureaucracy is too large for presidents to pressure all key players
 (D) All of the above

159. The modern president is seen as the party leader because

 (A) the executive branch has significant power
 (B) the president can effectively deliver messages to the public
 (C) of the power and influence of the bully pulpit
 (D) All of the above

160. The president can set policy by which of the following methods?

(A) Executive appointments
(B) Public speeches
(C) Meetings with congressional leaders
(D) Executive orders

161. The nationalization of public policy by Franklin D. Roosevelt's New Deal was perhaps inevitable due to

(A) the inability of state governments to provide services
(B) the Supreme Court's interpretation of powers of the commerce clause
(C) the larger resources of the federal government
(D) All of the above

162. Lyndon B. Johnson's expansion of domestic public policy in the 1960s was called

(A) the New Frontier
(B) the Great Society
(C) the New Federalism
(D) the New Freedom

163. The executive branch has the most control for setting the policy agenda because

(A) the president has the bully pulpit
(B) Congress concentrates on legislation
(C) Congress does not control funding
(D) the national bureaucracy is rooted in the executive branch

164. The U.S. Postal Service is the best representation of what type of bureaucracy?

(A) Independent government corporation
(B) Independent regulatory commission
(C) Independent executive agency
(D) Independent congressional agency

165. Policymaking has changed with the growth of executive power because

(A) unified rather than divided government is needed
(B) administrative mechanisms now produce significant changes
(C) states now receive their ideas from the federal government
(D) new policy only needs the cooperation of the president and a few governors

166. The executive branch directs the bureaucracy and its policies, but it has to make sure it complies with

(A) the House
(B) the Senate
(C) both houses of Congress
(D) the judiciary

CHAPTER 5

The Judiciary and Policy Making

167. In the United States v. Lopez case, what congressional power did the Supreme Court rule Congress exceeded when attempting to keep handguns away from schools?

(A) The Commerce Clause
(B) The Necessary and Proper clause
(C) The Establishment Clause
(D) The ability to tax

168. Judicial review—the ability of the Supreme Court to decide the constitutionality of laws—was established in which of the following cases?

(A) *Gibbons v. Ogden*
(B) *McCulloch v. Maryland*
(C) *Marbury v. Madison*
(D) *Scott v. Sandford*

169. Until the Civil War, the court concentrated on issues related to

(A) economics
(B) federal versus state authority
(C) presidential power
(D) national expansion

170. *McCulloch v. Maryland* was the first step in establishing national supremacy by

(A) overturning a national organization
(B) validating the necessary and proper clause
(C) affirming a presidential executive order
(D) reversing state law

171. During the second era of judicial review, from the end of the Civil War to the 1930s, the court concentrated on

(A) property rights
(B) civil rights
(C) civil liberties
(D) the role of the national government

172. Franklin D. Roosevelt tried to change the makeup of the Supreme Court by

(A) decreasing the number of justices
(B) changing the tenure of justices
(C) requiring presidential and congressional approval of decisions
(D) increasing the number of justices

173. Lower-court judges tend not to contradict the Supreme Court because

(A) a reversed decision is a defeat for a judge
(B) frequent reversals could damage a judge's reputation
(C) reversed decisions will bring greater scrutiny
(D) All of the above

174. Substantive judicial doctrine comprises decisions that

(A) are applied to government policy and future cases
(B) rely on precedents
(C) establish a boundary of federalism
(D) originate in state courts

175. Opinion writing by the Supreme Court has risen compared to other historical periods because

(A) the court stopped contesting the authority of Congress and the president on economic regulation
(B) party control of the White House changes
(C) justices want to make a name for themselves
(D) Both A and B

176. Judicial nominations are the reverse of legislative vetoes of the Supreme Court because the nominations

(A) reinstate judicial rulings
(B) confirm judicial precedent
(C) allow the elected branches to influence future judicial decisions
(D) are a positive action of constitutional practice

177. The most common way the elected branches seize statutory control from the Supreme Court is through

(A) legislative action
(B) constitutional amendments
(C) executive orders
(D) disregarding the ruling

178. If the president and Congress ignore a Supreme Court ruling,

(A) they are censured
(B) they do not face any consequences
(C) the ruling is enacted through an override
(D) they face possible impeachment

179. Judicial review allows the modern Supreme Court to act as

(A) the final authority on legislation
(B) the chief referee of the U.S. political system
(C) a guide to acceptable legislation
(D) the "keeper" of the Constitution

180. The judiciary has authority over the bureaucracy because it is independent and the courts

(A) have constitutional authority over government agencies
(B) treat the government differently than other parties in a lawsuit
(C) defend individual rights, which constrains government agencies
(D) decide on whether laws are legitimate

181. Which court case established the limits of presidential emergency authority?

(A) *Korematsu v. United States*
(B) *Youngstown Sheet and Tube Company v. Sawyer*
(C) *Hamdi v. Rumsfeld*
(D) *Rasul v. Bush*

182. The post-*Youngstown* judicial interpretation of presidential power reflects all of the following political features of the modern American presidency EXCEPT

(A) presidential efforts to control bureaucratic discretion
(B) the increase of divided government
(C) the growth of the federal debt
(D) increased judicial activism

183. The federal judiciary has confined separation of powers interpretations to

(A) advice to the executive
(B) communications on congressional realignment of the appellate system
(C) cases initiated by private parties or the government
(D) congressional acts

184. The legitimacy of the Supreme Court rests on the fact that it

(A) does not have any set standards to its interpretation on the separation of powers
(B) either favors both legislative and executive branches or neither when making decisions
(C) overrides the actions of a strong executive
(D) can overturn congressional actions

185. Over the past 50 years, the Supreme Court has been reluctant to make strong decisions against the use of military force or foreign relations because

(A) it does not want to create new policy
(B) these are political questions best resolved by Congress and the president
(C) little precedent has been established
(D) there is a jurisdictional question to the issue

186. The Supreme Court has been more aggressive in its adjudication of certain executive and congressional determinations, such as immigration policy, because

(A) they represent a gray area between foreign and domestic policy
(B) the court believes this is an executive authority
(C) the court believes this is a legislative authority
(D) the court believes the judiciary has authority

187. Bureaucracies that mix legislative and executive powers have led the Supreme Court to adopt a highly formal separation of powers doctrine due to
    (A) the power it gives the executive branch
    (B) the violation of Article I of the Constitution
    (C) the power it gives the legislative branch
    (D) the power it has over the federal budget

188. The president has been subjected to judicial controls and procedures
    (A) to limit the reach of executive authority
    (B) to deny absolute executive privilege
    (C) to rectify the problems caused by divided government
    (D) because Congress has been ineffective at checking the executive branch

189. Until the New Deal in the 1930s, judicial attitudes toward the U.S. political process were republican, meaning
    (A) they favored Republicans
    (B) they protected property from legislative majorities
    (C) they favored the institutions of democracy
    (D) they wanted to expand political freedoms

190. The judiciary can influence policy on all governmental levels through
    (A) trials
    (B) decisions
    (C) interpretation of the law
    (D) Supreme Court rulings

CHAPTER 6

Networking Within the Federal Government

191. When bureaucratic agency staff, members of Congress, and organized interest groups form alliances, they are commonly referred to as

(A) institutional bonds
(B) politically expedient partnerships
(C) iron triangles
(D) policy linkages

192. Iron triangles control policy in their domains

(A) with the full oversight of Congress
(B) with full public support
(C) with no oversight in operations
(D) with coordination by the public and large agencies

193. Iron triangles and captured agencies exist only as long as

(A) everyone agrees with their actions
(B) they continue to receive funding
(C) they stay under the political radar
(D) they maintain their coalitions

194. Due to increased judiciary rulings that created procedural standards on bureaucracies, Congress passed the

(A) Sarbanes-Oxley Act
(B) Patriot Act
(C) Administrative Procedure Act (APA)
(D) McCain-Feingold Act

195. Red tape, the colloquialism used for *bureaucracy*, exists because

(A) it allows both the beneficiary and bureaucrat to see progress, no matter how slow
(B) it prevents Congress from having control over the administration
(C) it allows bureaucratic output to be measured
(D) it allows agency accomplishment to be measured

196. Bureaucracies are perpetually trying to be reformed into more efficient systems but to little avail because of

(A) the needs of the public
(B) the need for regulation
(C) the nature of government
(D) the size of the federal bureaucracy

197. Since the 1950s, what characteristic of government has had a significant impact on the relationship of the legislative and executive branches and the bureaucracy?

(A) Divided government
(B) Redistricting
(C) More transparency
(D) The use of committees

198. Congress and the president have been empowered by the federal courts through

(A) a reluctance to render decisive rulings on their actions
(B) a consistent understanding of each branch's constitutional authority
(C) a broad interpretation of what the legislative and executive branches' powers are
(D) a strict, narrow interpretation of powers

199. Legislative gridlock often occurs due to the multiple veto opportunities in the checks and balances system and causes which of the following problems?

(A) A variety of provisions must be added that favor narrow constituencies.
(B) It tips the balance of power toward the president.
(C) It tips the balance of power toward Congress.
(D) It tips the balance of power toward the bureaucracy.

200. The inclusion of numerous constituencies to avoid gridlock leads to compromises where

(A) few major acts pursue a consistent purpose

(B) gridlock is generally solved with legislation that seeks balance between the president and Congress

(C) the president has the advantage in negotiating

(D) Congress has the advantage in negotiating

201. Policy disagreements among the bureaucracy's political principals creates a control problem because

(A) the bureaucracy requires guidance from the president

(B) the bureaucracy requires guidance from Congress

(C) the bureaucracy acts independently from the president or Congress

(D) the bureaucracy pits Congress against the president over policy

202. The control problems of policy implementation among different parts of the government are solved by all of the following EXCEPT

(A) ex ante controls (controls created before implementation)

(B) ex post controls (controls created after implementation)

(C) legislation

(D) bureaucratic review

203. The institutionalized presidency is a form of ex ante control on policy implementation because

(A) the president can set policy in his or her favor

(B) the president can surround himself or herself with loyal advisors

(C) Congress has a disproportionate amount of government control

(D) the president creates the bureaucracies

204. The recent history of the political bureaucratic system has demonstrated a rise in political extremism due to

(A) fractured public opinion

(B) divided government

(C) the increased authority of bureaucracies

(D) a vast increase in the number of issues with which the government deals

205. Under President George W. Bush, policy power rested with the president because

(A) of the terrorist attacks of September 11, 2001

(B) of increased polarization of the parties and a Republican party majority in Congress

(C) the Bush administration took unprecedented steps to control policy from the executive branch

(D) of the wars in Iraq and Afghanistan

206. Which of the following groups was created by government bureaucrats to help interested parties?

(A) The National Organization for Women (NOW)
(B) The National Association for the Advancement of Colored People (NAACP)
(C) Mothers Against Drunk Driving (MADD)
(D) The Business Roundtable

207. A controversial fact about many interest groups regarding their relationships with legislators is that

(A) they often draft significant portions of legislative bills
(B) they often employ legislative staffers
(C) they are the liaisons with the executive branch
(D) All of the above

208. Political scientist David Mayhew discovered that divided government produced legislative results that were _____ of unified government.

(A) similar to those
(B) better than those
(C) worse than those
(D) different than those

209. According to David Mayhew, Congress's performance may be shaped by

(A) presidential cycles
(B) broader issues
(C) political knowledge
(D) All of the above

210. Woodrow Wilson believed that the president could harness party organization and public opinion to

(A) control Congress
(B) control the bureaucracy
(C) create public policy
(D) use the party to influence public opinion and public opinion to manage the party

211. A distinctive feature of the presidency after Franklin Roosevelt has been

(A) increased cooperation with Congress
(B) the diminution of cabinet independence in policy matters
(C) decreased cooperation with Congress
(D) the need to deal with divided government

212. What effect does the information the media provide have on government?

    (A) It significantly alters the relationship between government and governed.

    (B) It does not impact the government's relationship with the people.

    (C) It alters the behavior of elected officials.

    (D) It limits what can be accomplished.

213. Media regulation is beneficial to news outlets because it

    (A) keeps government operating within a set of rules

    (B) stabilizes a marketplace and reinforces the status quo against new competitors

    (C) allows the media more access to all branches of government

    (D) prevents the modern presidency from dominating news coverage

214. Government at all levels indirectly subsidizes the news media by

    (A) doing all the legwork of writing reports, documenting data, and keeping records

    (B) organizing bureaucracies

    (C) coordinating activities at the local, state, and national levels

    (D) providing information for favorable coverage

215. The creation of the government press secretary was necessary because

    (A) the workings of the government remained relatively secret

    (B) there was an increasing demand on elected officials for news coverage

    (C) politicians wanted to hide their activities

    (D) elected officials wanted to add another layer between press and politician

216. Public policy decisions are made overwhelmingly by

    (A) Congress

    (B) the president

    (C) the judiciary

    (D) the bureaucracy

217. Formula distributions of federal money are a favorable method of policy formation because

    (A) money is distributed evenly

    (B) one region does not benefit at the cost of another

    (C) no special projects are given to any particular district

    (D) earmarks are not used

218. Earmarks do not require _____ as formula distributions do in setting policy.

(A) committee approval
(B) trade-offs
(C) a public roll-call vote
(D) agreement from the executive branch

219. Interest groups utilize the parochialism of Congress to influence policy agendas by highlighting

(A) the voting record of members
(B) the different effects national policy may have on different regions
(C) the action of committees
(D) certain issues in which they are interested

220. National bureaucracies are important in setting policy agendas because

(A) the president gives them the power to do so
(B) Congress gives them the power to do so
(C) they possess the necessary expertise in a certain area
(D) they often come up with necessary innovations that pertain to issues

221. Elected officials in the legislative and executive branches delegate authority to the bureaucracy to

(A) increase efficient delivery of services to the public
(B) avoid the responsibility of poor bureaucratic action
(C) address the myriad citizen demands made on the government
(D) offset judicial rulings that may affect legislation

222. The threefold problem with delegation in controlling the bureaucracy comprises bureaucratic expertise, multiple reporting structure, and

(A) political turnover
(B) public opinion
(C) judicial review
(D) bureaucratic competition

223. The information problems associated with bureaucracy are complexity of information and

(A) executive branch interference
(B) the preference of bureaucratic agencies
(C) congressional oversight
(D) the proliferation of interest groups

224. A policy network is

(A) a group of individuals in unrelated fields who are connected by an issue

(B) the committees in Congress and bureaucracies involved in a public policy area

(C) the interest groups and government officials who work together on particular issues

(D) the executive bureaucracy, Congress, and lobbyists involved in a policy area

225. Policy networks help facilitate

(A) connections between politicians and the public

(B) relationships between states and the federal government on certain issues

(C) an explanation of the salient points of an issue to both the public and the government

(D) the nationwide messaging of issues

226. Policy networks help interest groups establish trust with government officials by

(A) keeping up communication

(B) responding to proposals

(C) gathering intelligence

(D) All of the above

227. Policy networks are successful because they

(A) plan legislative strategy

(B) motivate politicians by reducing the political price for getting involved

(C) assemble legislative coalitions

(D) draft legislation

228. Policy networks can influence change through

(A) litigation

(B) organization

(C) media outreach

(D) polling

PART 3

Civil Liberties and Civil Rights

CHAPTER 7

Civil Liberties: Incorporation of the 14th Amendment

229. In the Supreme Court case McDonald v. Chicago the Supreme Court incorporated the right to

(A) Keep and bear arms
(B) Grand juries
(C) Speedy and public trials
(D) Retain a witness in your favor

230. For nearly a century, the Supreme Court's ruling in _____ set a precedent that kept the Bill of Rights from being applied to state law.

(A) *Barron v. Baltimore*
(B) *Gibbons v. Ogden*
(C) *Marbury v. Madison*
(D) *McCulloch v. Maryland*

231. The Supreme Court first applied First Amendment protections to the states in the *Gitlow v. New York* ruling by finding that

(A) states cannot control the press
(B) states cannot limit religious activity without due process
(C) states cannot interfere with free speech
(D) states cannot automatically keep people from assembling

232. The Bill of Rights guaranteed rights and liberties for citizens by proscribing what the federal government could do. The Fourteenth Amendment brought those proscriptions to state action through

(A) legislation
(B) incorporation
(C) federalism
(D) judicial review

233. The due process clause of the Fourteenth Amendment means that

(A) the state cannot deny rights and liberties
(B) everyone is equal
(C) equality is determined on a case-by-case basis
(D) legally established procedures must be used if rights and liberties are denied

234. The Fourteenth Amendment's incorporation of the Bill of Rights to apply to states has been selective rather than total because

(A) state enforcement of criminal law should remain autonomous
(B) incorporation is too vague
(C) the guarantees of the Bill of Rights are not clear and indisputable
(D) fundamental fairness was too subjective

235. The due process clause of the Fourteenth Amendment has been incorporated into which amendments in the Bill of Rights?

(A) First, Second, Third, Fourth, Fifth, and Eighth
(B) First, Second, Fourth, Fifth, Sixth, and Eighth
(C) First, Fourth, Fifth, Sixth, Seventh, and Eighth
(D) First, Third, Fifth, Sixth, Seventh, and Eighth

CHAPTER 8

Civil Liberties: 1st, 2nd, & 4th Amendments

236. The Supreme Court struck down public school prayer in this case

- (A) Hazelwood v. Kuhlmeier
- (B) Tinker v. Des Moines
- (C) Gitlow v. New York
- (D) Engel v. Vitale

237. In the case N.Y Times v. the United States (1971) the Supreme Court reestablished this two century rule in regards to the role between the press and federal government

- (A) Prior restraint
- (B) privacy
- (C) Using informants
- (D) Libel

238. The World War I case Schenck v. the United States created this famous Supreme Court test

- (A) Litmus test
- (B) Clear and present danger test
- (C) Lemon test
- (D) Privacy test

239. When the Supreme Court struck down Wisconsin's mandatory school attendance policy as a free exercise of religion violation in what case?

- (A) Engel v. Vitale
- (B) Wisconsin v. Yoder
- (C) Obergefell v. Hodges
- (D) Vernonia School District v. Acton

240. Public school students retain the right to political expression in what case?

(A) Mapp v. Ohio

(B) Engel v. Vitale

(C) Wisconsin v. Yoder

(D) Tinker v. Des Moines

241. What is the difference between civil rights and civil liberties?

(A) Rights are protections from government, and liberties are protections by government.

(B) Rights are protections by government, and liberties are protections from government.

(C) They are interchangeable with no difference.

(D) The government may not take away citizens' rights.

242. Trends in civil liberties litigation are attributable to the

(A) wording of new laws

(B) the shifting ideology of the Supreme Court

(C) the makeup of Congress

(D) presidential elections

243. The increase in the acceptance of substantive rights and liberties has been recognized due to _____ changes.

(A) economic

(B) political

(C) judicial

(D) cultural

244. *Schenck v. United States* established that speech posing a _____ was not protected by the First Amendment.

(A) risk to the government

(B) call to public acts of mayhem

(C) clear and present danger

(D) promotion of disloyalty

245. Civil liberties and civil rights are often not well defended when

(A) the nation is at war

(B) there is increased immigration

(C) there is a shift in political power

(D) the Supreme Court defers to Congress and the president

246. The clear and probable danger test, an addition to the clear and present danger test in *Schenck v. United States*, was introduced in

(A) *Mapp v. Ohio*
(B) *Texas v. Johnson*
(C) *Dennis v. United States*
(D) *Griswold v. Connecticut*

247. *Roth v. United States* issued a new doctrine regarding rights and liberties surrounding

(A) immigration
(B) obscenity
(C) flag burning
(D) draft dodging

248. *Miller v. California* held that, instead of applying a broad definition of obscenity, _____ should be responsible for deciding what is obscene.

(A) community boards
(B) law enforcement in each case
(C) state and local governments
(D) local courts

249. The rights and liberties connected to freedom of the press are often measured against the rights and liberties of

(A) the accused
(B) private citizens
(C) public officials
(D) civil litigants

250. The religious freedom Americans enjoy is due to the First Amendment's _____ and free exercise clause.

(A) elastic clause
(B) equal protection clause
(C) establishment clause
(D) take care clause

251. A law satisfies the establishment clause for religion if legislation

(A) advances but doesn't inhibit a religion
(B) has a secular legislative purpose
(C) doesn't purposely foster excessive government entanglement
(D) refrains from clear public endorsements

252. A significant, but now faded, Supreme Court precedent on the establishment clause was set in

(A) *Gideon v. Wainwright*
(B) *Furman v. Georgia*
(C) *Griswold v. Connecticut*
(D) *Lemon v. Kurtzman*

253. What was the pivotal Supreme Court decision banning prayer in public schools?

(A) *Betts v. Brady*
(B) *Wolf v. Colorado*
(C) *Benton v. Maryland*
(D) *Engel v. Vitale*

254. First Amendment protections include freedom of

(A) religion
(B) the press
(C) speech
(D) All of the above

255. The _____ Amendment prevents the government from making illegal searches and seizures.

(A) Third
(B) Fourth
(C) Fifth
(D) Sixth

256. *Griswold v. Connecticut* and *Roe v. Wade* are landmark Supreme Court cases because they established privacy claims through

(A) the legality of contraception
(B) abortion
(C) reproductive rights
(D) All of the above

257. Rights and liberties regarding privacy have been interpreted to be at least partially guaranteed by the _____ Amendment.

(A) Fourth
(B) Fifth
(C) Seventh
(D) Ninth

258. The right to privacy, the constitutional basis for the Roe v. Wade case, was established in

(A) Planned Parenthood v. Casey
(B) Bowers v. Hardwick
(C) Miranda v. Arizona
(D) Griswold v. Connecticut

CHAPTER 9

Civil Liberties: Procedural Due Process

259. The right to an attorney in a criminal case was incorporated in this case

(A) Miranda v. Arizona
(B) Escobedo v. Illinois
(C) Gideon v. Wainright
(D) Mapp v. Ohio

260. Which of the following amendments pertain to the rights of the criminally accused?

(A) Third, Fourth, Fifth, and Sixth
(B) Third, Fourth, Fifth, and Seventh
(C) Fourth, Fifth, Sixth, and Eighth
(D) Third, Fourth, Fifth, and Seventh

261. Which of the following cases extended the exclusionary rule of evidence to include state law enforcement?

(A) *Baker v. Carr*
(B) *Furman v. Georgia*
(C) *Mapp v. Ohio*
(D) *Benton v. Maryland*

262. *Miranda v. Arizona* established that those accused of a crime have the Fifth Amendment right not to

(A) incriminate themselves
(B) be forced to go to trial without an attorney
(C) have an unwarranted search of their property
(D) go to trial without a jury

263. The historical reasoning for the Sixth Amendment's protections regarding jury trials stemmed from

(A) the Federalist belief that the accused was guilty until proven innocent

(B) violations against the colonists during the years leading up to the American Revolution

(C) the original practice of local magistrates deciding the fate of the accused

(D) a legal separation from English tradition

264. The most famous Supreme Court decision involving the Sixth Amendment guarantee of representation at trial was

(A) *Miranda v. Arizona*

(B) *Gideon v. Wainwright*

(C) *Furman v. Georgia*

(D) *Baker v. Carr*

265. *Furman v. Georgia* resulted in a majority of states writing statutes so the courts could continue to

(A) convict and sentence the mentally disabled

(B) consider evidence obtained without a warrant

(C) determine the size and composition of juries

(D) use the death penalty as punishment

266. One of the reasons criminal rights (those associated with the Fifth and Sixth Amendments) were not nationalized until the 1960s was

(A) the legal technicalities surrounding criminal trials

(B) the issues surrounding the language and interpretation of the amendments

(C) the exact nature of the rights of the accused

(D) All of the above

267. The right to privacy, although not explicitly mentioned in the Constitution, exists because of these implicit areas of protected privacy rights within the Constitution.

(A) Penumbras

(B) Interpretative clauses

(C) Implied liberties

(D) Focal points

268. The takings clause of the Fifth Amendment, otherwise known as eminent domain, has recently limited the claims of property owners in the Supreme Court's decision in

(A) *Betts v. Brady*
(B) *Heath v. Alabama*
(C) *Kelo v. City of New London*
(D) *Benton v. Maryland*

CHAPTER 10

Civil Rights: Equal Protection Under the Law

269. Equal protection is a prolific source of modern constitutional litigation because

- (A) it pertains to civil rights and civil liberties
- (B) more of these cases come to the court's attention
- (C) most legislation pertains to equal protection issues
- (D) executive orders often violate civil rights

270. In Brown v. the Board I the Supreme Court used what constitutional provision to strike down public school segregation

- (A) Article I's necessary and proper clause
- (B) Due Process clause of the 5th Amendment
- (C) Equal Protection Clause of the 14th Amendment
- (D) Establishment clause of the 1st Amendment

271. In terms of civil rights and liberties, a suspect classification is one

- (A) where legislators legitimately apply the law to a certain group of citizens
- (B) where judicial interpretation is questionable
- (C) where there is concern that legislation separates a class of people
- (D) where the law gives favor to a particular group

272. The strict scrutiny that affected "fundamental" rights or interests regarding equal protection was more profound on the development of civil rights and liberties because

- (A) it circumscribed legislative choices
- (B) it focused on voting
- (C) it focused on criminal appeals
- (D) All of the above

273. Under Chief Justice Warren Burger, the post-Warren Supreme Court's view on equal protection was

(A) a discontent with the two-tier formulation of equal protection
(B) a willingness to use the clause as an interventionist tool
(C) an avoidance of the strict scrutiny language of the Warren court's equal protection
(D) All of the above

274. The Burger court maintained equal protection for fundamental interest classifications in

(A) voting and ballot access
(B) sexual harassment
(C) racial profiling
(D) gay marriage

275. One way the modern (from the 1990s into the twenty-first century) court's equal protection interpretation has changed is that

(A) civil rights are not as protected
(B) law enforcement action is more acceptable
(C) there is a new concentration on citizenship
(D) the deferential approach does not automatically overturn statutes

276. The major case that helped further split North and South prior to the Civil War was

(A) *Miranda v. Arizona*
(B) *Scott v. Sandford*
(C) the *Amistad* decision
(D) *South Carolina v. United States*

277. Reconstruction was instituted by a Republican Congress to
_____ and ensure civil rights in the South.

(A) prevent all African Americans from voting
(B) create an orderly way for Southern states to be readmitted to the Union
(C) guarantee a victory in the next presidential election
(D) give African Americans the right to vote

278. "Separate but equal" to justify state-sponsored segregation came from which of the following cases?

(A) *Plessy v. Ferguson*
(B) *Baker v. Carr*
(C) *Miranda v. Arizona*
(D) *Mapp v. Ohio*

279. *Plessy* was overturned by

(A) *Mapp v. Ohio*
(B) *Scott v. Sandford*
(C) *Brown v. Board of Education of Topeka*
(D) *Kelo v. City of New London*

280. *Regents of the University of California v. Bakke* limited the reach of

(A) equal protection
(B) the federal government
(C) affirmative action
(D) workplace discrimination

281. Judicial interpretation of civil liberties and civil rights has extended from the rights of African Americans to those of

(A) women
(B) the disabled
(C) homosexuals
(D) everyone

282. In the Supreme Court case *U.S. v. Morrison* the Court struck down a federal gun restriction law around schools because

(A) It violated the 2nd Amendment
(B) The commerce clause of Article I didn't apply to gun regulation
(C) It imposed on the states' ability to regulate guns
(D) It imposed on local governments abilities to regulate guns

283. A recent landmark case for gay civil rights citing privacy protection for individuals is

(A) *Mapp v. Ohio*
(B) *Baker v. Carr*
(C) *Lawrence v. Texas*
(D) *Miranda v. Arizona*

284. Judicial interpretation on all federal levels of the _____ has been inconsistent, keeping a national policy muddled.

(A) Civil Rights Act of 1957
(B) Civil Rights Act of 1964
(C) Family and Medical Leave Act
(D) Americans with Disabilities Act

285. Ultimately, civil rights for all were achieved by judicial interpretation as well as

(A) a national majority using the full force of the federal government
(B) the imposition of heavy taxes on segregated businesses
(C) tax incentives to segregated businesses
(D) a shift in the demographics of the population

286. Unlike civil rights, the judicial advancement of civil liberties has required

(A) considerations of cultural differences
(B) deference to the intent of legislation
(C) a shift in the demographics of the population
(D) a check on majorities that assert their prerogatives over individuals

287. Civil liberties and civil rights have developed through the interpretation of the _____ Amendment.

(A) Thirteenth
(B) Fourteenth
(C) Fifteenth
(D) Sixteenth

288. The Fourteenth Amendment was the linchpin in the legislation that began

(A) the Civil War
(B) the Gilded Age
(C) the end of slavery
(D) Reconstruction

289. The original interpretation of equal protection in the Fourteenth Amendment is that legislative statute reasonably relates to a

(A) legislative purpose
(B) right ensured by the Bill of Rights
(C) decision by state legislatures
(D) guarantee of equal rights

290. The Supreme Court, led by Chief Justice _____, began to use equal protection as a tool to overturn discriminatory legislation.

(A) Warren Burger
(B) William Rehnquist
(C) Earl Warren
(D) John Roberts

291. The *Slaughterhouse Cases* prevented the development of interpretation on which clause of the Fourteenth Amendment?

(A) Due process
(B) Equal protection
(C) Necessary and proper
(D) Privileges and immunities

292. The Fourteenth Amendment's main purpose was to legally settle

(A) citizenship
(B) racial discrimination
(C) voting rights
(D) Jim Crow laws

293. The National Association for the Advancement of Colored People (NAACP) effectively used the Fourteenth Amendment to end

(A) discrimination in all forms
(B) state-mandated segregation
(C) the Supreme Court's use of racial classifications
(D) the use of the strict scrutiny standard of racial classifications

294. The Fourteenth Amendment has been used to categorize gender as a suspect class because

(A) of the feminist movement
(B) of increased awareness of sexual harassment
(C) of more women in the workforce
(D) of the Supreme Court's changing attitude toward gender classification

295. *Korematsu v. United States* was a case involving race as a suspect class that
- (A) upheld discrimination by the government based on race, regardless of a strict scrutiny test
- (B) found that the federal government could not discriminate, even in times of war
- (C) did not recognize the application of the Fourteenth Amendment in times of war
- (D) did not believe that pressing public necessity was enough to curtail the rights of certain individuals

296. The Supreme Court has used which of the following standards in cases involving gender discrimination?
- (A) Strict scrutiny
- (B) Deferential scrutiny
- (C) Partial scrutiny
- (D) Heightened intermediate scrutiny

297. The Supreme Court's decision to implement desegregation of public schools throughout the United States "with all deliberate speed" came with
- (A) Brown v. the Board I
- (B) Brown v. the Board II
- (C) Swann v. Charlotte-Mecklenburg
- (D) The Scottsboro Boys case

298. The Supreme Court has refused to grant heightened scrutiny and subsequent Fourteenth Amendment protection to which of the following groups?
- (A) The mentally ill
- (B) Women
- (C) Illegitimate children
- (D) The poor

299. Opponents of the Equal Rights Amendment (ERA) claimed the protection for women, through proper interpretation, can be found in the
- (A) The 5th Amendment's due process clause
- (B) The 14th Amendment's due process clause
- (C) The 14th Amendment's equal protection clause
- (D) The 19th Amendment providing women the right to vote

300. The problem the Supreme Court faces in determining whether a neutral law is actually discriminatory is the proof of

(A) underlying prejudice
(B) historical discrimination
(C) purposeful discrimination
(D) regional prejudice and discrimination

301. The Supreme Court has ruled that the Fourteenth Amendment does not apply only to correcting a decisional process that caused discrimination like segregation; it also applies to

(A) intent
(B) an underlying purpose
(C) public perceptions
(D) achievement of a certain result

302. A recent controversy surrounding the Fourteenth Amendment naturalization provision involves

(A) immigration
(B) citizenship
(C) gay marriage
(D) terrorism

303. The Supreme Court has found that voting represents a(n)

(A) unquestionable right
(B) pivotal component of democracy
(C) foundational principle
(D) fundamental interest

304. Using the Fourteenth Amendment to restrain the private sector is controversial because

(A) the Supreme Court has had difficulty creating a clear line of reasoning for it
(B) the amendment is aimed at government action
(C) the amendment originally pertained only to racial discrimination
(D) All of the above

305. The Supreme Court has used the Fourteenth Amendment's equal protection to strike down what action associated with government?

(A) Lobbying
(B) Redistricting
(C) Campaign finance reform
(D) Political action committees

306. For nearly a century, the Fourteenth Amendment was not considered successful because

(A) Jim Crow laws existed in the South
(B) the South was a segregated society
(C) former slaves were predominantly tied to the South
(D) All of the above

307. Section 5 under the Fourteenth Amendment allows Congress to make any laws necessary to carry out the amendment's provision, but the Supreme Court has found that

(A) this is not permissible
(B) the contradicts powers given the executive branch in Article II
(C) this allows Congress to cover private behavior as well
(D) only the judicial branch can enforce the amendment's provisions

308. The rationality requirement employed by the Supreme Court in cases involving equal protection sought to determine whether

(A) there was a connection between legislative classification and objectives
(B) rights were truly being protected
(C) the government could limit rights if there was a good reason
(D) equal protection applied to every citizen in all situations

309. In which case did the Supreme rule that redistricting districts on the basis of race must be subject to strict scrutiny?

(A) Shaw v. Reno
(B) Wesberry v. Sanders
(C) Baker v. Carr
(D) Clinton v. New York

PART ▶ 4

American Political Ideologies and Beliefs

CHAPTER 11

Political Socialization and Ideology

310. An example of a contradiction in what people believe the government should do economically for social welfare is

(A) lower taxes but less government action
(B) higher taxes but more government action
(C) lower taxes but more government action
(D) None of the above

311. Most Americans tend to take conservative positions on most social issues, but they respect

(A) government intervention
(B) government officials' positions on issues
(C) public advocates on the issues
(D) individual freedom

312. In the 20th century these events led to deep mistrust in the federal government:

(A) The Progressive Movement and World War I
(B) The Great Depression and World War II
(C) The Red Scare and the Cold War
(D) The Vietnam War and Watergate scandal

313. American citizens may show political ambivalence toward an issue because

(A) Most Americans identify as moderates
(B) Many Americans don't identify with party labels
(C) Interest groups are considered weak
(D) State party organizations are not very strong

314. Political donations were ruled to be a form of free speech in this case

(A) Schenck v. the United States
(B) Buckley v. Valeo
(C) N.Y. Times v. United States
(D) Citizens United v. FEC

315. All of the following explain general distrust in politicians in recent decades EXCEPT

   (A) The government wastes tax money.
   (B) Voters are better informed than in the past.
   (C) Politicians are controlled by special interests.
   (D) Politicians do not care about ordinary people.

316. The process of acquiring political attitudes is known as

   (A) political education
   (B) political culturalization
   (C) political understanding
   (D) political socialization

317. Political socialization takes place

   (A) during childhood and young adulthood
   (B) at the start of a career
   (C) when people begin to pay taxes
   (D) at the beginning of college

318. What group is considered to be the most reliable voting block?

   (A) Young people
   (B) Educated people
   (C) Senior citizens
   (D) Both B & C

319. Knowledge of political facts and leaders comes mostly from

   (A) family and friends
   (B) high school civics courses
   (C) the news media
   (D) political debates

320. Political ideologies are

   (A) a highly organized set of political attitudes
   (B) a highly organized set of political theories
   (C) a highly organized set of political opinions
   (D) a highly organized set of positions that politicians use to communicate with the public

321. Conservative ideology differs from liberal ideology in that conservatives

(A) have greater faith in the free market
(B) prefer less defense spending
(C) do not think the government should legislate morality
(D) believe that military force should not be used as often in international politics

322. Attitudes are not always defined by an allegiance to a particular ideology. Rather, individuals may use

(A) the opinions of family and friends
(B) information from news reports
(C) core values
(D) political party allegiance

323. Partisanship is

(A) identifying with a particular political party
(B) organizing your attitudes in line with a political party
(C) matching your core values with those of a party
(D) All of the above

324. Political attitudes introduce bias to the interpretation of political information because

(A) public opinion is never neutral
(B) people give more attention to information that confirms their beliefs
(C) such information is usually complex, and attitudes reduce it to one of two sides
(D) political parties tend to dictate attitudes

325. Individuals' political opinions often reflect collective experience rather than personal experience due to

(A) the influence of friends and family
(B) politics being the provision of collective goods
(C) few people expressing an opinion unless they know others share it
(D) their level of education

326. Until the middle of the 20th century most Americans received their political information from

(A) Political parties
(B) Radio
(C) Print media
(D) Word of mouth

327. Economic self-interest explains why those with low incomes are more liberal toward government programs, but _____ explains why those with high incomes are more liberal on social issues.

(A) culture
(B) community
(C) religion
(D) education

328. Which amendment was largely adopted because of a social movement?

(A) 16th Amendment
(B) 18th Amendment
(C) 21st Amendment
(D) 27th Amendment

329. Minority political beliefs differ from those of whites on a variety of issues due to

(A) life in different regions
(B) differences in cultural history
(C) a history of race-based discriminations
(D) separate sets of issues affecting each community

CHAPTER 12

Public Opinion and Polling

330. What type of polls are generally used to monitor elections?

   (A) Exit polls
   (B) Sample polls
   (C) Focus groups
   (D) Random polls

331. Citizens are most informed about politicians and issues by

   (A) activists defining the political agenda
   (B) the president defining the political agenda
   (C) the news media defining the political agenda
   (D) All of the above

332. What is the most common form of American political participation?

   (A) Joining an interest group
   (B) Making campaign contributions
   (C) Voting
   (D) Contracting an elected official

333. The use of _____ allows individuals to formulate opinions by relying on opinion leaders.

   (A) policy initiatives
   (B) TV, radio, and Internet personalities
   (C) cognitive shortcuts
   (D) polling data

334. The coherence of aggregate public opinion is based on

   (A) citizens' general knowledge about politics
   (B) the clearly defined positions of politicians
   (C) opinion leaders who combine information from various sources
   (D) the effectiveness of campaign advertising

335. According to political scientists, public opinions are

(A) opinions held by private individuals that governments find prudent to heed

(B) something that politicians need to mold if they are to be successful

(C) ideas that change over time and shape the directions of government

(D) the accurate representation of what the most important issues are

336. Two industries that developed due to the political importance of public opinion are

(A) news corporations and public relations

(B) scientific polling and public relations

(C) scientific polling and newswire services

(D) news corporations and scientific polling

337. Expressed public opinion reflects an organized and consistent manner of thinking, feeling, and reacting, otherwise known as political

(A) perspective

(B) attitude

(C) ideology

(D) stance

338. Public opinion is a powerful tool in the formation of policy because

(A) interest groups seek it

(B) politicians react to it

(C) presidents pander to it

(D) government action is influenced by it or influences it

339. Public opinion surrounding what social and moral issue helped shape legislative, executive, and judicial policy during the past 40 years?

(A) Gay marriage

(B) Abortion

(C) Sexual harassment

(D) Racial discrimination

340. How did public opinion change foreign policy after the end of the Cold War?

(A) The president became more responsive.

(B) Foreign policy was more varied and nuanced.

(C) Foreign policy became more aggressive in protecting American interests.

(D) Foreign policy became less aggressive in protecting American interests.

341. Aggregate public opinion is a more important measure of voter attitudes than individual public opinion because

(A) it truly represents the mood of the electorate
(B) it is more statistically accurate
(C) it better informs policy decisions
(D) it is stable and coherent over time

CHAPTER 13

Linkage Institutions and Public Perception

342. The news media's goals are often at odds with those of politicians because

(A) politicians want their actions and policies placed in a favorable light
(B) politicians do not trust the media
(C) the media don't trust politicians
(D) the media distort political messages because of their inherent bias

343. Politicians use the media to communicate with other politicians because

(A) going public with a position forces other politicians to act
(B) private conversations between politicians of opposing views are not always effective
(C) it allows the public to distinguish both sides of an issue
(D) All of the above

344. What is the term for when a politician sends an anonymous idea to see whether the public is receptive?

(A) Buoy
(B) Trial balloon
(C) Testing the waters
(D) Test flight

345. A discreet, news-making strategy available to all government officials is the

(A) off-the-record comment
(B) anonymous tip
(C) news leak
(D) press release

346. The beat system of newspaper and broadcast media has the following implications for news EXCEPT

(A) Beat reporters file dispatches regardless of newsworthiness.
(B) All government agencies are continuously covered.
(C) Pack journalism is more likely to occur.
(D) The president is usually covered the most.

347. The news media select what stories to cover and give the most press to

(A) stories that detail important public policy
(B) stories that explain politicians' positions on issues
(C) stories that are controversial and negative
(D) stories that detail the impact of legislation and presidential activity

348. The inherent tension between politicians and reporters is because

(A) each side would exploit the other if possible
(B) politicians feel journalists are out to get them
(C) journalists feel that politicians are the only true source of news
(D) it is a necessary partnership for both

349. The greatest consequence of strained relations between the press and politicians over events like Vietnam and Watergate is

(A) reporters' lack of access to politicians
(B) a proliferation of news leaks
(C) a credibility gap
(D) a distrust of both sides by the public

350. The public's poor perception of Congress is due to the nature of

(A) pluralism
(B) republicanism
(C) democracy
(D) a two-party system

351. The actions of members of Congress receive little attention from the general public because

(A) most people don't pay attention
(B) it is difficult to understand the political maneuvering
(C) making laws is all that matters to most citizens
(D) All of the above

352. All of the following are factors in the renewed partisanship of politics EXCEPT
    (A) political conflicts in Washington
    (B) a contentious national agenda
    (C) new ideologically driven activists
    (D) voter preferences

353. Politicians listen to interest groups because
    (A) they are not all popular or politically powerful
    (B) they are not informed on the issues
    (C) they are often a captive audience who must meet with constituents
    (D) they want to have an idea of public reaction before implementing programs

354. Some people see interest groups as a detriment because
    (A) they unduly influence politicians
    (B) they are responsible for policy gridlock
    (C) they enhance the power of Congress
    (D) they enhance the power of the president

355. Interest groups receive a great deal of public attention for all of the following reasons EXCEPT
    (A) They appear to have strong connections with politicians.
    (B) They are a relatively recent development to the political system.
    (C) They provide information and data to government agencies.
    (D) They use the media successfully.

356. According to political scientist David Truman, interest groups are a natural progression in American society because
    (A) the complexity of modern society has created more interests
    (B) the public has become more aware of political issues
    (C) the population continues to increase, creating more diversity
    (D) political rights are applied more evenly throughout society than in the past

357. The interests of marginalized groups in society (such as the mentally ill and the homeless) do not receive as much attention from politicians as the interests of industrial groups because the former groups

(A) lack any funding
(B) are not organized collectively around a narrow issue
(C) lack advocates in similar numbers to those for industrial interests
(D) benefit from charity as much as they do from legislation

358. A major force among interest groups for affecting change within the institutions of government is

(A) focus groups
(B) public lobbyists
(C) social movements
(D) public awareness initiatives

359. Congress is affected by media coverage because

(A) it does not allow congressional members to make private deals with fellow legislators
(B) it exposes all of Congress's activities
(C) the increase in coverage actually reduces substantive information delivered to the public
(D) it focuses only on certain issues

360. Although seemingly contentious, the relationship between the media and government officials ultimately

(A) maximizes their cooperation to meet the demands placed on them
(B) rests on trust
(C) is one-sided in favor of the media
(D) is one-sided in favor of the government

361. News organizations serve as a resource and _____ to presidents.

(A) fact checker
(B) partner
(C) relief from pressure
(D) source of pressure

362. The relationship between the media and government officials is personal, but it is more institutional due to
    (A) the number of reporters with whom an official must meet
    (B) the irrelevance of who the individuals in the political and media positions are
    (C) the structure of the government and news organizations
    (D) the public being the ultimate audience for each group

363. The media's demands for timely and accurate information serve all of the following purposes EXCEPT
    (A) making sure the government remains transparent
    (B) providing the public with necessary facts about government actions
    (C) meeting the needs of the public to form opinions
    (D) preventing public officials from having the time to craft their own news stories

364. The media link the public with government officials by
    (A) maintaining objective standards
    (B) carrying information between the public and the government
    (C) exposing corruption
    (D) detailing policy

365. Which of the following represents the media's basic responsibility of informing the public?
    (A) Detailing the activities of a corrupt politician
    (B) Looking back on an official's career
    (C) Criticizing a bureaucratic agency
    (D) Explaining what officials are doing, as well as official policies and goals

366. All of the following are reasons the government impacts the press EXCEPT
    (A) Government protects the media as an essential part of republican government.
    (B) Government provides information to news organizations through publicly funded press liaisons.
    (C) Government regulates certain media such as public broadcast stations.
    (D) Government facilitates alliances with key players who are formulating public policy.

367. The most consistent government support the media receives comes from the

(A) executive branch
(B) legislative branch
(C) judicial branch
(D) bureaucracy

368. In political science terms what is the term used for the bridge between the people and policy institutions?

(A) Arching institutions
(B) Linkage Institutions
(C) Intergovernmental institutions
(D) Federal agencies

369. The American Association of Retired Persons (AARP) is an example of an interest group that benefits from public opinion because

(A) it is the largest member organization of its kind
(B) it has great financial resources
(C) it markets itself successfully
(D) it has a specific focus

370. Public opinion influence on policy sets a limit on interest group effects because

(A) no member of Congress wants to seem to put interest groups ahead of the public good
(B) harnessing opinion can raise the most money
(C) public opinion frames messages better
(D) interest groups are disliked by the general public

371. Public opinion is inversely proportional to interest group influence on public policy due to

(A) parochialism
(B) political self-interest
(C) interests of geographic regions
(D) All of the above

PART 5

Political Participation

CHAPTER 14

Parties in the American Political System

372. All of the following were consequences of the fracturing of the New Deal party alignments EXCEPT

(A) Voters became indifferent to political parties.
(B) Congressional incumbents had more electoral advantage.
(C) Divided government became common.
(D) "Ticket splitting" decreased.

373. House and Senate members from the same state and party do not necessarily have the same political views due to

(A) constituency differences
(B) different responsibilities to the party
(C) varying connections to interest groups
(D) their message to the media

374. The lack of distinction between the partisan and ideological motivations of members of Congress in policymaking is largely due to

(A) contributions from interest groups
(B) the narrow focus of public policy
(C) party leaders creating policy that represents shared ideological goals
(D) feedback from constituents

375. Belonging to a political party helps deliver specific policy goals because

(A) Congress can work with the same party in the executive branch
(B) the party in control of the executive branch does not have as much impact on policy
(C) a party message is easier to disseminate to the public
(D) having a common stake in collective action facilitates the coordination of agenda items

376. Party politics is an important identifier for voters because

(A) it allows them to express themselves more easily
(B) it is an automatic organization of like-minded individuals
(C) past performance is a better criterion than future promises for preferred results
(D) political attitudes are validated for the individual

377. Political party affiliation remains a strong connection to what voters believe about government because

(A) cumulative experience may strengthen or weaken allegiance to a party
(B) it is an easy way to evaluate political situations
(C) voters tend to vote emotionally and strategically
(D) Both A and B

378. The primary incentive for the creation and continuation of political parties is

(A) to organize so as to win majorities in multiple settings
(B) to allow ideas and issues to coalesce around a central structure
(C) to formulate coalitions to pass legislation
(D) to gain control of the machinery of government

379. Political parties first developed in the United States when

(A) leaders in Congress with opposing visions began competing for legislative votes
(B) George Washington realized they were the best method for executing his agenda
(C) local citizens realized their political voice would be heard if they were better organized
(D) the Constitution was being ratified

380. Thomas Jefferson was the founder of the Democratic Republicans, or Jeffersonians, due to his opposition to which Federalist leader?

(A) George Washington
(B) John Jay
(C) Alexander Hamilton
(D) John Adams

381. Political parties build stable legislative and electoral alliances by

(A) creating coalitions of interests
(B) enabling national officials to coerce local officials
(C) establishing a central agreement of shared interests or values
(D) undermining the efforts of political opponents

382. The cohesive, organized structure of political parties is designed primarily to

    (A) mobilize voters

    (B) streamline messages

    (C) ensure that local members follow national leaders

    (D) enact legislation

383. Successful political parties continually develop

    (A) new electoral technologies

    (B) arguments around key issues

    (C) connections between the regional and national levels

    (D) effective legislation

384. Political parties use labels, messaging, and issues to organize members of the party in order to

    (A) offer voters cues as to where politicians stand on issues

    (B) ensure collective responsibility for the party's success

    (C) differentiate themselves from opponents

    (D) All of the above

385. An alternative to the winner-take-all system of American elections that would undermine the two-party system is

    (A) regional representation

    (B) inclusive representation

    (C) proportional representation

    (D) national representation

386. The organization of a two-party system benefits from federalism because

    (A) national leaders cannot maintain the diverse local coalitions

    (B) the parties' strengths lie in their uniformity from regional to national levels

    (C) the autonomy of the state and national government allows political parties to tailor objectives according to region

    (D) the spheres of influence of local and national leaders can remain separate to avoid alienating constituents in one region through support of constituents in another region

387. The Democratic Party was created by assembling a political network with the purpose of electing President _____.

(A) Andrew Jackson
(B) Martin Van Buren
(C) John Quincy Adams
(D) James Monroe

388. The creation of national party conventions in the early 1830s allowed broader participation in nominating presidential candidates and in

(A) increasing the number of presidential candidates
(B) forcing the House of Representatives to decide more presidential contests
(C) reducing the political power of the states
(D) establishing organized two-party competition for offices at all government levels

389. Prior to Progressive Era reforms, political parties maintained control at the local level through

(A) cooperation with authorities
(B) communication with national leaders
(C) patronage
(D) None of the above

390. Modern political parties cannot run party machines that control all aspects of electoral outcomes because of which of the following reforms?

(A) The primary system
(B) The Australian ballot
(C) Civil Service reform
(D) Tighter registration laws

391. Progressive Era reforms to political parties ended the party machine structure and caused which of the following consequences?

(A) Higher voter turnout
(B) Lower voter turnout
(C) Diversity among issues depending on the group
(D) Higher voter turnout among the poor and uneducated

392. Political parties make mass democracy possible because they do all of the following EXCEPT

(A) recruit and train leaders
(B) foster political participation
(C) organize the activities of government
(D) forge public opinion via elections

393. Candidate-centered rather than party-centered politics flourished in twentieth-century American politics because

(A) political parties no longer controlled nominations
(B) population movement out of the cities weakened the party machine
(C) new election laws prevented third parties
(D) there was no longer a need to package candidates

394. National party conventions are still important to electoral politics because they continue to

(A) showcase the best candidate
(B) strengthen party coalitions
(C) empower party leaders
(D) give voice to party activists

395. Congressional votes along party lines declined after the turn of the twentieth century, and ticket splitting became commonplace due to

(A) increased voter turnout among immigrants
(B) the migration of people out of the cities
(C) Progressive Era reforms
(D) the formation of new political alliances

396. The political actions of legislators are primarily governed by

(A) party politics
(B) parochialism
(C) national interests
(D) interest groups

397. Congressional members tie their political fortunes to their parties because

(A) voters view parties as the best indicator of candidate performance
(B) there is no advantage to being independent
(C) they want the best committee assignments
(D) the party connects them with better campaign financing

398. Government operates through the party system because

(A) that was the Founding Fathers' intent
(B) parties facilitate collective action
(C) parties give citizens more of a voice in politics
(D) parties allow easier, more fluid negotiation of legislation

399. For most of the twentieth century, political parties were seen as necessary because they

(A) helped formulate ideas about government
(B) were essential to the stability of democratic life
(C) organized the legislative and executive branches
(D) created strong political leaders

400. Until the 1990s, unified party control of government was preferred because

(A) it made the political climate less contentious
(B) that was how it had been for most of the nation's history since the Civil War
(C) it provided an additional bridge between the president and Congress, helping to avoid gridlock
(D) policies could be better regulated and administered

401. Party politics are currently polarized, which limits the opportunity for significant legislation because

(A) they represent a divided government between the president and Congress
(B) politicians are trying to attract the most voters to their side
(C) there is no ideological center
(D) there is a lack of communication between the major parties

402. When a political party comes into the majority after an election, it

(A) tries to energize the electorate
(B) strengthens the ties among branches
(C) loosens the ties among branches
(D) acts as though the voters have issued a mandate for a change in policy

403. For political parties, elections matter in terms of

(A) shaping public opinion
(B) shaping the array of policy views within and between the two parties
(C) formulating political strategy
(D) determining the strength of the president

404. Polarization between parties is debilitating and demoralizing for the minority party because of the difficulty of achieving bipartisanship and

(A) the lack of executive cooperation
(B) the public perception of ineffectiveness
(C) the lack of incentive to compromise on legislation
(D) the negative media attention

405. The formation of the first American parties occurred due to

(A) policy disputes
(B) logistics
(C) the need for legislative victories
(D) public opinion

406. A voter turnout of less than 10 percent for the election of 1820 clearly demonstrated

(A) how important parties are in mobilizing voters
(B) that James Monroe did not have a serious challenge in his reelection bid
(C) that the North and South were already beginning to come apart
(D) the influence of a strong opposition even when the opposition has no viable candidate

407. The Republican Party is anomalous in American political party history because

(A) it was formed over one issue
(B) it won national prominence right away
(C) it successfully challenged the two-party system
(D) it was purely national with no state affiliations at first

408. The national shift to the Democratic Party after the 1932 election of Franklin D. Roosevelt

(A) was the culmination of a 20-year trend
(B) permanently changed the federal bureaucracy
(C) was due to the strength of party organization
(D) was due to Herbert Hoover's ineffectual leadership

409. Current control of political parties rests with

(A) party officials
(B) interest groups
(C) elected officials
(D) congressional leaders

410. The two-party system arises from
- (A) differences in public opinion
- (B) strategy in a winner-take-all system
- (C) the separation of powers
- (D) legislation limiting third parties

411. The professional, business-like structure of today's national and state parties organize favored policy initiatives well because
- (A) there is little disagreement between national and local levels
- (B) the parties operate as one large corporate structure
- (C) the variation among regions produces a stronger basis for ongoing coordination
- (D) the parties can reach more voters more readily than in the past

412. The two-party system enables the government to function better than if one party dominated because
- (A) a two-party system can raise issues better
- (B) a two-party system prevents one party from restraining the policy preferences of large portions of the general population
- (C) a two-party system ensures that only the most pressing issues are discussed
- (D) a two-party system forces cooperation between major parties

413. Issues are raised in the U.S. political system through party allegiances because
- (A) the two-party system raises issues and creates rational solutions
- (B) there is no other way to raise issues
- (C) interest groups have little say
- (D) the parties are the manifestation of citizens' desires

414. The two-party system allows policy issues to filter down from the national level by
- (A) coordinating party efforts in the federal system
- (B) adjusting the national issue to fit local concerns
- (C) advancing local candidates to national prominence
- (D) conducting party activity based on public policy

415. Major party leaders influence the policy process by
- (A) negotiating with the executive branch
- (B) negotiating with agencies
- (C) reacting to judicial decisions
- (D) shaping the overall budget

CHAPTER 15

Campaigns, Elections, and Money

416. In Presidential elections years voters tend to focus in on:

(A) Current foreign affairs
(B) Social issues
(C) The President's stance on abortion
(D) The status of the economy

417. The major reason for the decline in voter turnout in the past 40 years has been

(A) a decline in eligible voters
(B) apathy regarding once-important issues
(C) an increase in the diversity of the population
(D) a decline in mobilization efforts by parties and organized groups

418. The benefits of elections are _____ benefits. Therefore, citizens can enjoy the payoffs without having voted.

(A) collective
(B) political
(C) economic
(D) social

419. All of the following are reasons the elderly are such an important voting bloc EXCEPT

(A) They have a distaste for taxes.
(B) They distrust the government.
(C) They are dependent on government retirement programs.
(D) They are informed about issues affecting them.

420. Politicians pay close attention to group differences (such as race, gender, income) because

(A) they help formulate positions
(B) they determine coalition-building strategies
(C) they are important in winning elections
(D) All of the above

421. Which of the following issues is important enough to create single-issue voters?

(A) Taxes
(B) Education
(C) Gun control
(D) Social spending

422. Regular, free, competitive elections allow

(A) citizens to choose their leaders
(B) citizens to be heard by elected officials interested in remaining in office
(C) coalitions to be formed to affect political outcomes
(D) All of the above

423. According to studies, the strongest factors that influence voter turnout are

(A) age and race
(B) age and gender
(C) education and race
(D) age and education

424. According to scholars the decline in voter participation appears to be because of

(A) Jim Crow laws
(B) Cumbersome voter registration
(C) Work obligations
(D) Inability to get to polling stations

425. All of the following give incumbents seeking reelection an advantage EXCEPT

(A) a proven track record
(B) name recognition
(C) affiliation with a party out of fear
(D) substantial campaign finances

426. Negative campaigning is effective because it

(A) is more memorable in voters' minds
(B) exploits voter doubt in the opposing candidate
(C) showcases the opposing candidate's flaws
(D) All of the above

427. Campaign money is regulated because of all of the following EXCEPT

(A) Taxpayers partially finance presidential campaigns.

(B) Candidates need to keep track of what their opponents are spending.

(C) Private financing leads to suspicion of politicians serving their donors.

(D) Pursuit of money can discredit electoral victory.

428. Regarding campaign financing, the Federal Election Campaign Act (FECA) of 1971

(A) restricted public funding for all federal campaigns

(B) allowed unlimited contribution amounts

(C) required full reporting of contributions and expenditures

(D) set deadlines for when candidates had to announce their intentions

429. FECA was challenged in which Supreme Court case?

(A) *Buckley v. Valeo*

(B) *Kelo v. City of New London*

(C) *Baker v. Carr*

(D) *Clinton v. City of New York*

430. For a citizen to run for office, he or she needs

(A) name recognition

(B) major party support

(C) money

(D) campaign staff

431. The ultimate barrier to a more egalitarian campaign finance system is the

(A) unequal distribution of wealth

(B) desire of elected officials to change the system

(C) power of special interest groups

(D) First Amendment

432. The most important information shortcut voters use to make predictions about a candidate is his or her

(A) voting record

(B) personal experience

(C) issue platform

(D) party label

433. All of the following are components that voters do *not* like about the electoral process EXCEPT

(A) interest groups
(B) money
(C) the basic institutions of government
(D) media coverage

434. Government officials and opinion leaders criticize voter _____ as part of the problem with the electoral process.

(A) apathy
(B) fickleness
(C) loyalty
(D) ignorance

435. Public opinion shapes congressional elections, which, in turn,

(A) shape legislation
(B) create the need for more bureaucracy
(C) alter representation
(D) solidify relationships with other political institutions

436. In candidate-centered elections, public opinion and voter response are more important factors because

(A) candidates want to be leaders in their party
(B) catering to voters will give candidates greater committee assignments
(C) the party in power will view the election as a mandate
(D) the incentive to be a responsive politician is greater than the incentive to be collectively responsible

437. In party-centered elections, public opinion and voter response are less important factors because

(A) the party comes before constituent needs if they are in conflict
(B) candidate response to voter concerns remains important
(C) policy is influenced more by the executive branch
(D) party leaders receive their cues from public opinion and voters rather than individual candidates

438. Public opinion and voter efficacy can be affected significantly by

(A) the media
(B) redistricting
(C) congressional action
(D) presidential action

439. The rise of candidate-centered elections has led to a sharp increase in

(A) voter turnout
(B) legislation
(C) media coverage
(D) campaign spending

440. Redistricting during the past 30 years has allowed each major party to

(A) reach more voters
(B) create safer districts for incumbents
(C) make congressional races more competitive
(D) make inroads in historically one-party districts

441. Public opinion and voter turnout are most influenced by

(A) the media
(B) policy initiatives
(C) crisis situations
(D) well-funded campaigns

442. Incumbency is a primary factor to electoral success because

(A) it allows politicians to position themselves as unbeatable
(B) the media will follow incumbents' actions
(C) voter apathy tends toward the status quo
(D) challengers do not have the name recognition

443. Staying in good standing with voters is the best way for a politician to avoid

(A) missing the needs of his or her constituency
(B) misinterpreting the desire for a policy initiative
(C) facing a strong challenger in the next election
(D) provoking voter discontent

444. Seats in the House of Representatives occasionally go uncontested because

(A) candidates and activists anticipate possible outcomes
(B) there are no viable challengers
(C) the incumbent has too much money
(D) party politics dominate congressional elections

445. Representation by anticipation is not a perfect indicator of electoral outcomes due to the fact that

(A) challengers may run regardless of the odds
(B) voters may not appreciate their preferences being anticipated
(C) policy issues may change perspectives
(D) legislation may affect voter opinion

446. To attract voters, office seekers must create a campaign that has

(A) endorsements
(B) media attention
(C) favorable public opinion
(D) a theme or message

447. Negative campaigning, although disliked by the electorate, is effective because

(A) it erodes the trust and regard the public may have for a candidate
(B) it ensures that all issues will be discussed during the campaign
(C) it always changes public opinion
(D) it is seen as a positive for the candidate issuing the negative statements

448. The most effective way to win elections is

(A) to earn the trust of the electorate
(B) to make sure your voters come out to the polls while your opponent's voters do not
(C) to help form public opinion
(D) to use campaign advertising to affect public perception

449. The Bipartisan Campaign Reform Act (BCRA) is more commonly referred to as

(A) the Sarbanes-Oxley Act
(B) the Patriot Act
(C) the McCain-Feingold Act
(D) the American Recovery and Reinvestment Act

450. Although favored by the public, the idea of term limits has drawbacks, including

(A) diminished incentives for politicians to form strong ties with constituents

(B) overzealous representatives trying to push through far-reaching legislation

(C) a lack of voter awareness of new candidates

(D) the loss of experienced political leaders who are replaced by more inexperienced politicians

451. Public policy is influenced by elections because

(A) a new Congress means new laws

(B) a new president means new policy focus and initiatives

(C) elections represent the opinion of the citizenry

(D) elections are the only opportunities the people have to be heard

452. Major reconfigurations in American popular voting patterns are called

(A) authorizing elections

(B) deauthorizing elections

(C) realignment elections

(D) reapportionment elections

453. An authorizing election affects public policy by

(A) granting power to incumbents to maintain policies

(B) granting power to challengers to bring about reform

(C) confirming the public's choice for the incumbent president

(D) fully supporting the efforts of one of the major parties

454. Modern presidential campaigns require up-to-the-minute awareness of public opinion best provided by

(A) focus groups

(B) public meetings

(C) town hall–style debates

(D) candidate forums

455. Elections and public policy are strongly linked because elections resolve

(A) leadership questions

(B) who will be the local and state representatives

(C) who will be the national representatives

(D) coordination problems

CHAPTER 16

The Media, Interest Groups and the American Public

456. The link of interest groups and the political process often causes

(A) more citizens to be heard
(B) a stronger relationship between citizens and elected officials
(C) policy gridlock
(D) the enactment of more policies through legislation

457. The most frequent method that interest groups use to influence policy is

(A) cultivating relationships with elected officials
(B) petitioning the offices of elected officials
(C) providing expert testimony on a subject
(D) pitting elected officials against each other for popular support

458. Lobbying is

(A) the introduction of a subject to be considered by elected officials
(B) the exertion of influence on the general public as to what issues are important
(C) the activity of elected officials trying to gain more votes for their policy interests
(D) a direct appeal to lawmakers for policy support by a narrowly focused interest group

459. From the earliest days of the United States, observers such as James Madison and Alexis de Tocqueville thought interest groups could harm the political process because

(A) they undermined free speech and association
(B) disrupted public order and good government
(C) prevented the most important issues from being discussed
(D) demonstrated the result of too much free speech and association on the political process

460. Interest groups are successful in American politics because

(A) groups can access the political process in numerous ways
(B) elected officials must build broad-based coalitions
(C) they were indirectly created by the structure of the Constitution
(D) Both A and B

461. Special interest groups tend to have more representation in government politics than others because of

(A) organizational resources
(B) the interest of the American public
(C) the coverage given by the media
(D) the attention given by the president

462. Small special interest groups often successfully lobby elected officials on policy because

(A) voters do not spend time finding out about the issue
(B) if voters find out, they may not take the time to oppose the policy
(C) the small group is motivated to affect policy
(D) All of the above

463. Citizens who contribute to interest groups without worrying whether it will make an appreciable difference do so because of

(A) moral incentives
(B) selective incentives
(C) personal incentives
(D) economic incentives

464. Large special interest groups use selective incentives to get people to participate because these incentives

(A) are benefits that can be denied to those who do not contribute
(B) are easier to manage due to the organization's size
(C) work better when dealing with large numbers of people
(D) are easier to administer and beneficial in terms of cost to the organization

465. K Street in Washington D.C. in well-known because one can find

(A) House of Representatives offices
(B) Senate Offices
(C) Major Interest groups offices
(D) Most federal bureaucracies

466. Special interests that rely on dues and individual contributions for financial support prefer when political opposition to their cause is in power because

(A) membership and money increase
(B) they can make a better argument for their cause
(C) more media attention is given to the issue
(D) it is easier to create a strategy to promote issues

467. Technological advancements have allowed interest groups to proliferate because

(A) they can reach and maintain more members
(B) it is easier for members to remain connected without sacrificing too much time
(C) there are more issues than ever before
(D) more voters are concerned about more issues than ever before

468. The federal government has encouraged the growth of interest groups by

(A) creating more public policy legislation throughout the twentieth century
(B) suggesting the creation of interest groups to form a built-in constituency
(C) loosening the rules for lobbying
(D) taking over more authority from the states

469. An interest group's primary responsibility is to

(A) educate the public on an issue
(B) court administrators for special privileges
(C) create talking points for politicians to use
(D) gain as many members as possible to make its issue more politically important

470. Special interest groups represent numerous issues, and large groups split into smaller organizations because

(A) the policy process becomes fragmented
(B) new issues divide existing organizations
(C) links between problems are more transparent
(D) All of the above

471. Political action committees (PACs) can encompass all of the following categories EXCEPT

(A) labor
(B) corporate
(C) trade/membership/health
(D) professional

472. PACs with a narrow policy objective seek to influence public policy by

(A) electing new members to government bodies
(B) currying favor with committees dealing with the issues
(C) recruiting more donations because of the policy interest
(D) distributing money to other like-minded interest groups

473. PACs with broad ideological agendas seek influence by

(A) playing the role of political insider with knowledge of the issue
(B) generally favoring incumbents to maintain policy advantages
(C) adopting an outsider strategy to unseat incumbents
(D) persuading elected officials to change their policies

474. PAC contributions to members of Congress ensure

(A) favorable legislative outcomes
(B) predictable voting among politicians
(C) priority for specific issues
(D) access to the legislative process

475. All of the following are barriers to PAC influence EXCEPT

(A) Voters reject PAC influence on politics.
(B) Issues have two sides, so competing PAC interests may cancel each other out.
(C) Other more lucrative sources can easily finance campaigns.
(D) Politicians need to win elections, not just raise money.

476. The role of the media focused on the competitive side of politics is known as:
(A) Scorekeeper
(B) Watchdog
(C) Gatekeeper
(D) Muckraker

477. The role of the media focused on determining what is newsworthy is known as:
    (A) Scorekeeper
    (B) Watchdog
    (C) Gatekeeper
    (D) Muckraker

478. The logic of lobbying and interest groups rests on the idea that
    (A) politicians want to hear from various sources
    (B) politicians need money for campaigns
    (C) there is strength in numbers
    (D) communication between the government and the governed is vital for democracy

479. Professional lobbying has increased with modern representative government because
    (A) people hire lobbyists to advance their cause to the legislature or executive
    (B) modern bureaucracies are complex, and experts are needed to navigate the procedures
    (C) lobbyists' expertise allows them to influence legislation on complex subjects
    (D) All of the above

480. The greatest threat to an interest group's influence is
    (A) the appeal of a similar group to the same supporters
    (B) the loss of sympathetic politicians
    (C) a strong opponent of the group's agenda
    (D) public apathy

481. Interest groups provide political players with two types of information: political and
    (A) economic
    (B) social
    (C) cultural
    (D) technical

482. The Administrative Procedure Act requires that

(A) interest groups be recognized as representing a vital interest
(B) all agency rules and regulations be published in the *Federal Register*
(C) all meetings between agencies and interest groups be made public
(D) all politicians disclose who their lobbyist contacts are

483. Public demonstrations offer certain interest groups a powerful tool for affecting change because such demonstrations

(A) solidify a group's cause
(B) provide a reward that is worth the risk
(C) demonstrate the commitment of a large portion of society
(D) help in messaging

484. Grassroots lobbying is

(A) a type of lobbying done by the rank and file of an interest group
(B) usually a regional effort
(C) only used as a last resort
(D) a way to defray costs

485. Large interest groups utilize grassroots lobbying because it

(A) is easier to communicate on the local level
(B) is more targeted to the relevant voters of an area
(C) formulates messaging
(D) inconspicuously mobilizes members to reiterate demands to politicians

486. Political action committees (PACs) form a(n) _____ part of current interest group activity.

(A) large
(B) small
(C) highly political
(D) influential

487. Government officials and the media spend time and resources on

(A) providing the public with necessary information
(B) cultivating relationships
(C) making use of each other's presence for their own benefit
(D) sharing information

488. For the media, informing the public has led to

(A) a more public practice of government
(B) more strained relationships between the government and the media
(C) increased public awareness of policy issues
(D) a loss of control of the political process by elected officials

489. In addition to information, the media offer assessments on legislation that can

(A) influence public opinion
(B) influence how elected officials vote on the measure
(C) change the focus of the legislation
(D) develop into a source of information for the news

490. The media also play a role in

(A) informing government officials about issues of which they are unaware
(B) the relationship among the branches of government
(C) delegating the coverage of government's response to stories
(D) determining the success of election campaigns

491. A vital service the media provide to government officials and the public is

(A) connecting officials with constituents
(B) conducting public opinion polls
(C) interpreting policy
(D) empowering interest groups

492. Interest groups and public officials also need the media to provide

(A) an explanation of opponents' positions
(B) an overview of the current political climate
(C) an early warning system for emerging issues and problems
(D) mediation between politicians and interest groups

493. The press is connected to public policy because it

(A) shapes it
(B) interprets it
(C) delivers it
(D) disseminates it

494. To lobby Congress successfully for legislation regarding an issue, the issue has to have

    (A) national relevance
    (B) national support
    (C) strong political support
    (D) All of the above

495. The influence of interest groups on the policy process is limited due to all of the following EXCEPT

    (A) Most public policy issues do not generate advantages for narrow interests.
    (B) Influence on members of Congress is limited by public opinion.
    (C) Influence on members of Congress is limited by members' policy beliefs.
    (D) Influence on members of Congress is limited by the committees on which they serve.

496. The political leverage of interest groups to make policy rests with money contributions and

    (A) expertise
    (B) the influence of public opinion
    (C) connection with the executive
    (D) legislative input

497. The only way to determine the focus of an interest group's policy initiative is to

    (A) observe the voting patterns of certain members of Congress
    (B) analyze the costs and benefits involved
    (C) observe the actions of certain bureaucracies
    (D) analyze the actions of specific committees

498. Legislative examples of excessive influence of a narrow interest group are

    (A) federal mandates
    (B) tax loopholes
    (C) block grants
    (D) matching grants

499. An interest group's greatest opportunity for policymaking success is to

  (A) donate money to a campaign
  (B) provide expertise
  (C) draft legislation
  (D) frame issues as constituency matters

500. The influence of interest groups wanes when

  (A) a policy issue is no longer relevant in public opinion
  (B) a policy issue is more relevant in public opinion
  (C) a policy issue runs out of money
  (D) a policy issue conflicts with executive branch preferences

ANSWERS

PART 1 FOUNDATIONS OF AMERICAN DEMOCRACY
Chapter 1: Constitutional Foundations

1. (D) The Articles of Confederation created a weak central government that could not collect taxes. Further, all states were responsible for their own actions, and there was an inherent coordination problem in defending the nation if one or more states were attacked, as there was no standing army. All the other answers are either facets or criticisms of the Constitution.

2. (D) The major tax, the Stamp Act, ended the long-standing policy of salutary neglect. Prior to the Stamp Act England allowed its thirteen American colonies to grow economically and politically. The enforcement of the Stamp Act changed all of this. After this enforcement of this tax the British imposed their governmental will upon the colonies. This created colonial dissent eventually leading to the American Revolution.

3. (A) Daniel Shays led a rebellion in central Massachusetts against the taxes being levied against the farmers in the area. Most, including Shays, were ill-paid revolutionary veterans who felt abused by the state governments. The rebellion's initial success of disrupting local and state government caused concern for most other states that were in a similar situation.

4. (A) The other answers listed were definitely systematic problems created by the Articles. However the exportation of goods was not—the thirteen states were already an agrarian power exporting numerous agricultural goods.

5. (D) The legislatures were concerned that another Shays's Rebellion could happen in their own states and responded by trying to ensure that the citizenry would not revolt. Such a response further eroded government authority and wreaked havoc with local and state economies.

6. (B) Federalism, the sharing of political power between the national government and state governments, was created by the Constitution. Although not explicitly listed in the original Constitution, it was further clarified with the passing of the Tenth Amendment and is a cornerstone of our American political system.

7. (D) Alexander Hamilton was perhaps the strongest proponent of a strong central government and became the leader of the Federalist Party that emerged after ratification. His focus was economic strength, but he believed that all other aspects were connected to economics and held equal importance on the international stage.

8. (D) The Anti-Federalists' major theoretical objection was that only local democracy could empower the citizenry and that the United States was too diverse even then to be ruled by one set of laws from a remote central government.

9. (A) Alexander Hamilton and John Jay were New York delegates to the Constitutional Convention, and along with James Madison's state of Virginia, New York was the most important state to ratify the Constitution. The Constitution could still have been ratified without the wealthiest, most populous states, but it would not have had much political clout.

10. (C) While all of these answers can be argued to be correct, it is the structure and function of government that is the focus of the articles of the Constitution. The amendments and the government's practical operation derive from the creation of the system of checks and balances and federalism in the Constitution's structure.

11. (B) The Confederation Congress had no means of collecting taxes uniformly and therefore had no means of providing national defense or any service required of a national government. The debts incurred by the states varied, and some states were able to pay back debts sooner than others.

12. (C) The commerce clause has allowed the federal government to reach into areas ranging from shipping to broadcast television. The clause does not apply to taxation, but like all federal legislation, any commerce provision supersedes state law. Congress uses the clause to nationalize policy that may affect interstate commerce, which has been interpreted broadly across the legislative spectrum.

13. (B) Article I, Section 8 lists Congress's enumerated powers. They range from declaring war to coining money. The last power listed is the necessary and proper clause, or elastic clause, which states that Congress has the power to expand its responsibility legislatively as needed.

14. (B) *Frequent* may be a misleading term, as there have been only 27 amendments; however, all amendments except Prohibition have occurred through the method in answer B. Answers A and C represent parts of the other ways that amendments can be passed, and Answer D is not a proscribed method.

15. (C) The clearly defined roles of each branch, along with the separation of their powers, provide its authority. Answers A, B, and D are also connected to the separation of powers, but only because each branch's role is clearly defined.

16. (D) Due to the Founding Fathers' concern about a powerful central government, taxation rests with the House of Representatives because that is the body that most closely represents the people.

17. (C) James Madison, known as the Father of the Constitution, proposed the Virginia Plan at the beginning of the Constitutional Convention. It is the foundation of our legislative structure, because it created a national legislature that was separate from state governments. Although it was heavily modified, the seeds of federalism and national legislative authority existed within the plan.

18. (D) The New Jersey Plan was an alternative to James Madison's Virginia Plan that said the national government would not be based on population but that all states would have the same number of representatives.

19. (B) Congress's enumerated powers are discussed in question 13. The other sections pertain to the structure and responsibilities affiliated with representatives.

20. (A) The direct election of senators took the power to choose senators away from state legislatures as originally proscribed in the Constitution and therefore changed the structure of federalism from exclusivity between states and national government to more overlap of responsibilities.

21. (B) Judicial review, the ability to declare laws unconstitutional, was created in the *Marbury* case. Answers A & D are judicial philosophies whereas answer C is the main function of the Supreme Court.

Chapter 2: Federalism, Checks and Balances, & Separation of Powers

22. (D) The Constitution does not explicitly mention state or local governments. The Tenth Amendment does say any power not found in the Constitution is given to the states or the people.

23. (A) Federalism works primarily because the national government and state governments have exclusive spheres of influence.

24. (C) Confederation and unitary are the only two true forms of government provided among the answers. Parliaments are unitary, and republicanism and democracy are more theoretical constructs. Because we have a bicameral legislature (two houses of Congress), we have one house that operates under a unitary structure based on representation and another that operates as a confederation, where all member states have equal representation.

25. (B) The Twelfth Amendment pertains to the election of a president and vice president and was created to correct the problems caused by the election of 1796, in which Thomas Jefferson became John Adams's vice president, even though they were of different political parties. This is not a federalism issue.

26. (A) One of four types of unfunded mandates, partial preemptions allow a state government or agency to administer a federally mandated program provided the state agency adheres to federal guidelines. An example would be a state air pollution policy.

27. (A) Although all of the above cases deal with voting or campaigns, answer A focuses with congressional reapportionment. The famous quote "One person, one vote" stems from this case.

28. (D) The increase in unfunded mandates in recent decades has created huge economic burdens for the states while also eroding their authority on historically local issues. The intent or purpose of these mandates may be benign, but they affect every state and represent a tremendous increase in the power and reach of the federal government.

29. (B) Matching grants are where the federal government promises to meet the funds spent by a state on some policy area. Because the state knows that it will receive matching funds, state officials are not as diligent in their accounting of where money is used. States do not have to pay the entire cost of their actions, so they take more risks in spending on programs and therefore are less careful in budgeting for such programs.

30. (D) Although different types of grants and funding, all of the answers shown are examples of how the federal government uses money as a means of getting the states to accomplish federal goals.

31. (C) As society gets more complex and the federal bureaucracy gets larger, state action in areas from education to health care may be used as examples for the nation as a whole. Sometimes this can translate well, and other times it can fail due to the vast regional differences among areas of the country. Demographics, climate, and economy are all factors that sometimes hinder the success of state programs on the national level, but in the "see what works" approach, it often leads to innovative programs being introduced.

32. (A) Even more than Franklin Roosevelt's New Deal, Lyndon Johnson's Great Society sought to nationalize many programs he believed were vital to the health of the nation. The Great Society was meant to be his legacy; it introduced Medicare and Medicaid, as well as a host of other government programs enforceable through federal grants. Unfortunately, due to the escalating conflict in Vietnam, his domestic policies were overshadowed during his time in office. Through the grants, the Great Society remains perhaps the largest expansion of federal authority in our nation's history.

33. (D) Franklin Roosevelt began the significant push toward nationalization by seizing the opportunity during our great fiscal crisis—the Great Depression. Through regulation of what states could and could not do or what they must provide, he forever changed the paradigm of federalism to a national perspective.

34. (B) Conditions of aid are guidelines a state or local government must follow in order to receive federal funding. This can include any type of grants or mandates.

35. (B) The Fourteenth Amendment is perhaps one of the most important amendments, because it extends civil rights and liberties to all states. Originally drafted to give freed slaves citizenship, it has been expanded to apply most of the Bill of Rights to state laws to prevent discrimination or denial of rights.

36. (C) This 1819 case disallowed state governments from levying taxes on federal institutions, in this instance, the Bank of the United States. McCulloch was the branch manager of the bank in Maryland and sued because new state taxes were preventing the branch from functioning properly—which was the state's intent. In his decision, Chief Justice John Marshall famously stated, "The power to tax is the power to destroy."

37. (A) Article VI in the Constitution states that in cases of conflict, the Constitution will overrule any state or local law.

38. (D) Block grants are lump-sum payments for a particular state action or item. They do not cause as much reckless spending on the part of the state as do matching grants; the state knows that once the money from a block grant is spent, there is no more. Thus, states budget costs much more effectively.

39. (C) Madison feared factions' negative effects on a republican system of government. However, factions almost immediately appeared and developed into what we know as political parties. No faction or group of people can hijack government action due to the number of elections we have, our checks and balances system, and the inherent structure of federalism.

40. (C) Locke's social contract theory, the idea that the people and government have an agreement, is prominent in early American political thought.

41. (D) Jefferson's Declaration of Independence is considered to be an explanation for the colonies break from England using Locke's rationale for severing the social contract.

42. (D) Both philosophers believed in limiting the reach and power of the government over its people. Locke promulgated the idea of natural rights, and Montesquieu believed in implementing a structure of government that did not place too much power in any one person or small group of people.

43. (A) John Locke believed in natural rights and that authority comes from the consent of the governed. This same influence, which had a profound effect on Thomas Jefferson as he helped draft the Declaration of Independence, exists to some degree in the structure of the Constitution to ensure that one area of government does not become too powerful.

44. (D) As noted earlier, the idea of an independent judiciary allows for a part of the government to remain separate from the politics and emotions of creating laws. Montesquieu did not necessarily advocate that the judiciary be the sole arbiter of laws, but by remaining independent, it was in a better position to interpret laws for the benefit of all.

45. (A) The social contract theory, a concept used to establish nations and governments, is the basis for all government units in the United States.

46. (B) Pluralism is the theory whereby all social interests in a political system freely compete for government attention and favor.

47. (B) Gerrymandering was named for Elbridge Gerry, a Massachusetts politician who became vice president under James Madison and sought to increase his electoral advantage by creating a congressional district based on political support and not geographic similarity.

48. (C) The president's position in the legislative process is to approve or veto a bill. Constitutionally, the president has no responsibility or influence on creating legislation. However, much has changed in nearly 225 years, and the president, mainly through proposing the federal budget as noted earlier, greatly influences the legislative agenda.

49. (D) The veto, by nature, is not a proactive power. It is meant to stop action, and it therefore has no power beyond its exercise. The president cannot edit a bill in order to sign it or write legislation of his or her own. Vetoes simply throw the process back to Congress to ultimately decide whether to start again or override the veto.

50. (B) As government has grown, so has the bureaucracy. This growth is due to the increased role and power of the president in making sure that the execution of laws takes place. Presidents set policy agendas and manage the agencies that help administer those policies.

51. (C) Article III details the powers and structure of the judicial branch.

52. (B) The term *limited jurisdiction* is misleading; federal courts hear a variety of cases, as many different legal questions fall under the umbrella of "federal questions." This is another way of saying "constitutional question regarding everything from government action to civil rights." Also, when citizens have a legal dispute with a citizen of another state, the federal courts get involved when the dispute involves more than $75,000.

53. (A) Lower courts receive and interpret Supreme Court decisions to guide them on how they should rule on similar cases in the future. These precedents are the foundation of legal reasoning in courts at all levels. When the Supreme Court issues an unclear or a muddled decision, it throws the lower courts into a state of confusion, because different courts will interpret the ruling differently. Fortunately, this situation is rare, and the Supreme Court's authority is intact because it typically provides solid legal reasoning.

54. (C) Only Congress has the authority to remove federal judges from the bench through impeachment proceedings.

55. (B) This is the official request by the Supreme Court to review the records of a case from a lower court, typically from the appellate level. The Supreme Court can grant or deny "cert" without need for explanation, but four justices are needed to grant cert.

56. (C) If there are many "friendly" briefs filed on behalf of the case at hand or the lead attorney for the government wishes to argue the case, it stands to reason that the case has some significance and a decision is desired. Justices can use this to gauge whether a case should be heard.

57. (C) If the decision that has been rendered is legally sufficient, there is no need to pursue it further, and the decision remains. This is procedural doctrine.

58. (D) Departmental theory is a general theory that recognizes the need for quick action by different branches of government and the need for viable policies to be put into effect to solve problems. Therefore, the executive and legislative branches can make decisions as to what is within their given authority without having to wait on a Supreme Court ruling that may not happen for years, if ever.

59. (D) In *Federalist* No. 10, James Madison warned against factions as creating a tyranny of the majority and believed political parties thwarted the intent of compromise that fostered good, strong government.

60. (C) The history of the interaction between state and national governments has been one of power struggle. The national government continues to win, but state governments are autonomous in many areas, and the struggle will continue as that is the nature of federalism.

61. (A) The national government can change a state's policy even if that policy affects no other state but conflicts with national guidelines or standards. Environmental issues are a prime example, with emission standards or tax incentives for business often nationalized to keep the playing field level.

62. (A) The states can appeal federal government decisions in federal court, which is primarily a creation of Congress. This represents the importance of judiciary independence, as the judiciary is beholden only to the law and not the power of the elected branches of the national government.

63. (D) In 1913, senators were first elected directly rather than appointed by state legislatures. From that point forward, senators acted as self-interested candidates who could make a political name for themselves rather than individuals who were highly protective of their state's position in the nation. When senators were appointed, the states came first and thus held some power over the activities of the national government.

64. (C) The supremacy clause was originally interpreted to delineate where national and state authority ended and began. As the national government has expanded its reach, there have been conflicts in national and state laws, which is why state laws began to be overturned when they conflicted with new national laws in the same areas.

65. (A) The Tenth Amendment is clear about state authority and was placed in the Bill of Rights to satisfy Anti-Federalist states' rights advocates. Unfortunately for the states, the amendment has largely been ignored, and national authority and power have increased.

66. (B) The Tenth Amendment has not had the impact intended because of the elastic, or necessary and proper, clause that allows Congress to do what it thinks necessary to meet the needs of the federal government. This has often been interpreted to mean that Congress can control actions previously controlled by the states.

67. (D) Public goods used to be controlled more by state governments, but as nationalization increased, the resources required for those public goods could not be met by the states. The New Deal was an example of new national government policies that could only be provided by the government—unemployment benefits, Social Security, and financial regulation.

68. (C) Federal mandates require all states to meet a specific standard, but there are also policies that affect only coastal states or farming states and that place a burden on those states to comply. They are compelled to do so by the Constitution, but that does not mean it is easy for them to meet national government requirements.

69. (A) The New Deal was the prime example of national government expansion that the states could not handle on their own and thus readily complied with requirements. The public demand for assistance was nationwide at this time, and Franklin Roosevelt's administration met that need. States were not inclined to oppose such widespread public opinion.

70. (A) The national government is the arbiter that settles differences among states. As the Constitution makes clear, state conflict is automatically the purview of the national government, but there will be certain instances where bordering states try to ignore this fact and attempt to settle their differences. The national government does not cede this authority to the states at any time.

71. (C) Public demand is difficult for elected officials to resist, and even if that means giving up certain responsibilities at the state level, state elected officials will bow to it. Pressure from the national government coupled with public opinion is a political force that is irresistible to those serving in public office on the state and local levels.

72. (C) The New Deal was unlike anything ever imagined previously. Due to the crisis of the Great Depression, Franklin D. Roosevelt seized control of huge swaths of government authority not originally given to the federal government. Its size and scope set the tone and parameters for the federal government to move forward.

73. (D) Collective action is a problem at any government level. As national government programs and bureaucracies continue to grow, the states are not in a position to oppose such action effectively. Thus the trend toward nationalization will continue.

74. (B) This is particularly true for welfare programs and other government services. No state wants an increase in the population that will require government assistance. If a state provides excellent benefits, then residents of other states will be attracted to relocate. An increase in population will cost the state more and probably change the benefit. To avoid this, states may try to offer the fewest possible benefits so their populations will not increase.

75. (D) Any of these answers are legitimate responses. However, when looking for the best answer, it comes down to whether states can avoid complying with a government regulation. Regardless of the outcome of a case, the states may realize that the cost for noncompliance is too great and eventually come under federal control as the national government's resources and organization are much better.

76. (A) State governments, through the state legislatures and governors, have to be more connected to the people living in the state. The national government cannot offer the same connection, because even House members have to keep in mind the activities of the national government when addressing the needs of their constituents.

77. (C) Programs like the New Deal and Great Society changed the political landscape and brought many state activities under federal control.

78. (D) Unlike Congress, the president has to represent everyone and also be concerned with policy implementation and international standing. Therefore, the president's attention is not focused on the interaction between state and national governments unless it conflicts with an initiative he or she is promoting.

79. (B) Mandates, in all their forms, are the way the federal government imposes its prerogatives on the states. States are forced to comply and often incur a heavy financial burden. Any federal funds offered are readily accepted, which in turn makes the states even more beholden to the federal government.

80. (C) It is much more difficult for states to coordinate action than it is for the federal government to do so; therefore even if states were opposed to the expansion of federal programs, they have no legitimate alternatives to offer.

81. (B) Cutthroat competition is limited among states—regulatory restriction is an example—because the federal government is typically involved in any part of society where states may try to compete. For instance, a state does not have the authority to lift environmental standards to attract industry because that is controlled by the federal government.

82. (A) The Constitution, as the law of the land, is the guide used by the Supreme Court. The Constitution is vague on many areas and does not address some issues at all. The business and focus of the Court is to apply the Constitution to every case that it hears to create case law to be followed in the future.

83. (B) The judiciary cannot be proactive in most instances, because it cannot take positions on policy unless it is deciding a case. Case law can adjust activities after the fact, but there is no recourse for the courts to address issues before they are legally challenged. This system works well and is part of the reason the independent judiciary has the authority and credibility to decide legal challenges to government action.

84. (D) The 5–4 decision in this case fell along political and ideological lines, with the conservative members outnumbering the liberal members of the Court by one justice. However, the election was settled, and even though many disagreed, the Court continued with its business and did not lose its credibility over one highly contested, politically vital decision.

85. (C) Although the federal government has wrested power from the states over the course of this country's history, the states are still the way the federal government reaches the American people. Any national program is administered through states, and state governments still provide the most direct actions that affect the citizenry.

86. (B) Federalism divides government between the states and the national government. Any national policy has to be crafted at the national level, but more than that, the national government has to ensure that all state governments comply with the Constitution. Any policy, state or national, that does not meet that criterion, must be changed. To make this change possible, effective national policies must be instituted.

87. (C) Elected officials are concerned with their own constituents. But as part of the national government, these regional issues rarely become larger than the areas where they exist. It does not benefit either party to focus on a regional concern and neglect other regions at the same time. Parties effectively stifle regional conflict so they do not damage their national agenda.

88. (C) Strict scrutiny holds to the language in the Constitution. If the Constitution does not reference it, then it is not constitutional. This view is also referred to as narrow scrutiny.

89. (D) The Supreme Court does not take its task lightly, and whenever possible, it will defer to Congress on the validity of legislation. The Court will overturn any law that is in violation of the Constitution, but it has realized that holding all legislation in narrow focus is as detrimental to the functioning of government as is any violation of constitutional provisions.

90. (D) Judges are supposed to be objective, but that does not mean they have no political preferences. These preferences create predictable reasoning from case to case and, over time, result in an established record of adjudication. These ideologies also signal to politicians which judges will rule to their liking if placed on the federal bench.

91. (D) Civil liberties are protected by the Supreme Court, which interprets the Constitution. All the responses given are aspects of the Court. The term *veto* is meant only to represent that the Court can overrule legislative and executive action, and the definition of citizens' rights in general derives from Supreme Court rulings.

92. (A) In the new American republic, McCulloch affirmed the federal government's supremacy over the states. When Maryland attempted to tax the federal bank, the Supreme Court ruled the state could not tax a federal institution and the "power to tax was the power to destroy."

93. (D) The only possibility among these answers is that elected officials on the national level will remain generally honest due to the fact that their efforts can be overturned by another branch. Presidential vetoes can be overridden by Congress, and legislation can be found unconstitutional, so officeholders are best served by remaining honest in their dealings with each other.

94. (A) The Supreme Court ultimately decides on the constitutionality of federal and state legislation. That is its primary power regarding checks and balances. The chief justice oversees the impeachment trial of the president, but the court is not consulted when legislation or executive orders are considered, nor is it involved in international treaties.

95. (D) Congress's power rests with the confirmation of federal judges. The executive branch nominates judges and executive appointments and negotiates treaties.

96. (A) The independence of our judiciary allows it, in theory, to operate beyond the consideration of everyday politics and render decisions based on law.

PART 2 INTERACTION AMONG BRANCHES OF GOVERNMENT

Chapter 3: Congress and Policy Making

97. (D) The length of the term actually allows senators to establish a more significant voting and performance record, as it is three times the length of a House term.

98. (A) The congressional committee system is a vital component to the legislative process, as it represents a division of labor that can assess and formulate opinions on the myriad of issues facing the national government in a limited amount of time. Through expert testimony and analysis, committees are able to put forth logical approaches to policy initiatives that the entire Congress can vote on.

99. (C) Party leaders, in the House more than the Senate, can decide what issues should come up for a vote. If legislation will not further their agendas, it is unlikely that there will be debate on the issue.

100. (B) Conflict resolution is the only way for congressional business to move forward. Although it appears to the general public that Congress does not do much, it actually does a significant amount, considering the tremendous number of political, economic, and social considerations it must weigh. The nature of Congress is contentious, as both parties struggle for political control, so conflict resolution is a must.

101. (D) Due to the yearly budget requirement, the House is perpetually pressed for time. If legislation needs time to pass, it may well be shelved for political expediency. If the budget is not passed, the government can shut down nonessential services, as happened with the budget impasse of 1995.

102. (A) The Rules Committee decides how bills will be debated on the floor of the House. Amendments to a bill are controlled by the Rules Committee, thus debate is stacked in the majority party's favor.

103. (D) Named after the "whipper-in" that keeps hounds together in a fox hunt, these representatives round up their party members to vote on legislation the way the party wants. They are the coordinators of the system, keeping all members of the party in line.

104. (D) Due to its size, unanimous consent agreements are how the Senate handles amendment and debate questions. These agreements are negotiated by party leadership and can include the order in which bills will be debated and how long the debate will be. However, only one member needs to object to thwart these agreements, and then the process must be put to a Senate vote.

105. (B) Party committees do not exist. Standing committees are permanent unless officially disbanded and pertain to continuous issues such as armed services. As of 2008, there were 20 standing committees in the House and 17 in the Senate. Select or special committees are temporary in nature and deal with a specific issue; however, there is no time limit placed on them, and some have continued to operate for decades. Ad hoc committees exist in the House and usually consist of issues requiring special or delicate political consideration, such as congressional pay raises. The Conference Committee is where the House and Senate come together to unify legislation and send it to the president.

106. (D) The public is often frustrated that more laws do not get passed, but the process is designed so that legislation is never rushed. After introduction, the bill is assigned to the appropriate committee for review. Most bills end here, as each committee has only so much time and cannot consider all legislation. If the bill is taken up, then the committee—or more likely, subcommittee—schedules hearings from experts on the issue. If the subcommittee acts on the bill, it edits it line by line and then sends it to the full committee, which upon accepting the bill, reports it to the full body (House or Senate). Then debate is scheduled; this is where the Rules Committee of the House has the power, as it decides whether the bill can have amendments or not. In the Senate, there is no Rules

Committee, but there is the filibuster that allows any member to delay a bill by maintaining the floor. After the debate and possible amendment, the bill is sent to the floor for a vote. Once this is done in both houses, a conference committee meets to reconcile the bill between the House and Senate so it can be sent to the president's desk. The order of the steps: introduction, assignment to committee, hearings, reports on the bill, schedule of debate, debate and amendment, the vote, in conference, to the president.

107. (D) From the Founding Fathers' desire to avoid emotionally charged legislation to the coalition building required to pass legislation, Congress does not overhaul existing systems easily. Usually incremental changes prevail, so there is a change over time. The status quo is beneficial because legislation that may end up not having the desired effect is not put in place all at once, and corrections can be made.

108. (B) Entitlements include items such as Medicare and Social Security—the two largest entitlements—for which the federal government is forced to budget. As the population ages, these two entitlements in particular are going to take up more and more of the federal budget. Entitlements also have to be paid by law, so the federal government does not have the option of avoiding payment or paying only a portion of the entitlement cost.

109. (D) The GAO provides members of Congress with vital information for their committees as legislation is considered and policy is initiated.

110. (A) Congressional hearings are an important opportunity for expert testimony to be heard and information gathered from numerous sources on a specific subject. They may appear tedious, and they often cover topics obscure to the general public, but they are invaluable in crafting legislation and establishing policy positions.

111. (C) Article I, Sections 8 and 9, of the Constitution provides Congress's enumerated powers and the powers denied Congress, respectively. In neither section, nor anywhere else, is Congress required to relinquish authority or control to any other part of government. Congress has chosen to do this voluntarily in order to work more efficiently.

112. (D) This act has not had a significant impact on the actions of the president. However, by implicitly stating that the president can deploy troops before letting Congress know, the law may give the president permission to conduct military missions without congressional approval.

113. (A) All of these answers can apply to Congress, but it is through investigations and bringing government activities to the public's attention that it has real power to limit the activities of the other branches.

114. (A) Shaping and controlling policy allows Congress to maintain its power in government. Because bureaucracies are the driving force of government policy practice, influencing bureaucratic action allows Congress to demonstrate its effectiveness to its constituents.

115. (A) The Supreme Court ruled that legislative vetoes, where Congress can reject an action taken by the president or executive agency, violated the meaning of the separation of powers because the veto belongs to the president. Congress has openly ignored this ruling and has continued to make legislative vetoes.

116. (C) As noted in the answer to question 230, Congress attempts to override executive action and authority through legislation. This violates the separation of powers between the executive and legislative branches. A corollary would be the line-item veto that has been found unconstitutional. The line-item veto is the reverse of the legislative veto in that it would allow the president to alter provisions of legislation rather than approving or vetoing the legislation as a whole—in effect, it would allow the executive branch to legislate.

117. (B) This is the Supreme Court case that negated the legislative veto and has subsequently been ignored by Congress. The case involved an immigrant who was granted a permanent work visa that was retroactively rescinded by an act of Congress, negating the executive branch's permission for Chadha to stay.

118. (C) Congressional committees oversee many government agencies. Any member on a specific committee with responsibility for agency oversight can affect change in that agency's position or actions in regard to policy.

119. (D) The statutory instructions that committee members use provide the basis for their authority. If statutes are detailed as to what can and cannot be done, then the committee members benefit because they know exactly the extent of their power and what they can accomplish. Usually, detailed statutes give more authority to committee members because there is no dispute about where their power rests.

120. (D) Congress possesses the power of the purse, and even though the president submits the budget, it is Congress that decides where the money is spent. If a party is in control rather than powerful individuals on committees, then where the money is spent will be of utmost importance to federal agencies.

121. (D) The legislative veto, although still employed by Congress despite the Supreme Court finding it unconstitutional in 1983, is a method that allows Congress to veto executive action. This can be interpreted as influencing or changing agency action, but the legislative veto is designed to halt presidential or executive bureaucratic action.

122. (A) House members can provide government services to their districts, but when a state receives funds from the federal government, senators usually receive the credit because they are the state's representatives on the national level.

123. (D) Congress is designed to maintain the status quo and often revises existing legislation rather than pass new sweeping reforms. That is not to say that reforms do not occur, but they are not part of the normal course of business. Therefore, there is not much controversy with most legislation.

124. (A) Committees, especially when they hold hearings, allow politicians the opportunity to state their positions clearly and reach the public directly. Through committee action in general, elected officials can outline a clear set of principles and positions in which they believe.

125. (D) Elected officials use committees to explain their stances on issues as well as to distance themselves from issues that are not popular. It is often as politically wise to show the public what you are against as it is to show what issues you support.

126. (B) Party and legislative influence are gained through the strategic use of committees. Issues can be promoted or tabled to satisfy constituents, and the party leadership has control over what legislation reaches the floor for debate. In a polarized or partisan environment, the party in control maintains a tighter grip on the levers of power because it does not want to cede any political ground to its opponent.

127. (D) Reducing the size of committees is equivalent to reducing power and authority. There is no logical political reason to do this, so committees grow instead of shrink.

128. (D) Committee members decide what issues are considered. It stands to reason that committees do not consider issues with which they do not agree, unless it is to make sure they are dismissed from further consideration.

129. (C) The Rules Committee is the committee that creates the rules and procedures on the order of legislation to be considered as well as whether it is possible to attach amendments to the legislation. Through this powerful committee, the majority party can set the legislative agenda in the House of Representatives.

130. (A) Congress can waive any action or policy in force if it has a compelling reason to do so. This may be done to give the agency in question time to adjust its policy or procedure, or it may be done for political means to win favor with voters or general public opinion.

131. (B) There are only 100 senators compared to 435 representatives. Further, a senator is one of only two statewide elected officials on the national level. However, it is the structure and practice of each chamber that provides senators with greater political power. One senator can hold up legislation and has more influence in negotiating policy and legislation given the rules of the Senate. This gives senators a more substantial position than their counterparts in the House.

132. (A) The congressional committee system is always a political struggle between the two major parties. But in a partisan and polarized political environment, neither party wants to cede any territory to the other side, slowing down a process that, by its nature, is not meant to be rushed.

Chapter 4: The Presidency, Bureaucracy and Policy Making

133. (A) Championed by Teddy Roosevelt, the bully pulpit is used by presidents to pursue their policy issues via the media. By using the media in this role the president hopes to use public opinion to pursue their agenda, like passing their legislation through Congress.

134. (A) During the era of the patronage system and party dominance, the president was little more than an administrator doling out appointments to keep the party faithful pleased. Parties were still fragmented, but offering a cabinet position to faction leaders smoothed over any animosity, as cabinet positions during this time were often stepping-stones to the presidency.

135. (B) As noted earlier, the presidency during the party patronage era was not the same powerful position it is today. The legislative agenda was not set by the president, but by the party that controlled the government. The president may have been the symbolic head of the party at the time, but he was not setting the agenda.

136. (D) The Constitution does not grant any of these powers to the president; it gives them to Congress. Also, the president must be a civilian, as the Founding Fathers were fearful of military leaders holding civilian political office.

137. (A) Treaties need to be ratified by the Senate. To avoid possible rejection by the Senate, the executive branch has developed and effectively used executive agreements, which are informal agreements between the president and a foreign country. They can pertain to trade agreements, military bases, and so on. This is an efficient way to conduct lesser business at a time when the government already has so much on its plate.

138. (B) Modern presidents have used executive privilege much more than their earlier predecessors did. This privilege is not mentioned in the Constitution, but presidents claim that it secures separation of powers, as some practices are purely executive in nature and can be decided by the president.

139. (D) Executive orders are a quick way for the president to affect policy without having to wait for legislation. There is little controversy over their use, as it streamlines the function of government. Executive orders carry the weight of law as long as they do not contradict existing law or the Constitution, and they can be overruled through legislation or judicial ruling.

140. (C) Although not found in the Constitution presidents can issue executive orders because of powers traditionally given to executive authority in history. At times presidents use executive orders to sidestep Congress or negate a court ruling.

141. (D) The federal bureaucracy is, for the most part, under the authority of the executive branch. Due to ever-increasing responsibilities, Congress has delegated much of bureaucratic responsibility to the president and the executive branch.

142. (A) The president submits the annual federal budget for Congress's consideration. This is done because the executive branch possesses the resources to research the numerous dimensions of the budget and compile one that meets the president's goals and agenda. Presidents can greatly influence the course of the government if they can pass a majority of the budgets they propose.

143. (B) The State of the Union address is required by the Constitution in that the president must report to Congress the government's current situation. Between the terms of

Thomas Jefferson and Woodrow Wilson, each president sent a letter to Congress providing the information. Since Wilson, the president has spoken before a joint session of Congress. Recent presidents use the opportunity to announce their political agendas for the coming year.

144. (B) Central clearance, developed during Franklin D. Roosevelt's administration, streamlines conflicting messages being issued by the burgeoning federal bureaucracy. It requires all bureaucratic information—from hearing testimony to annual reports—to be filtered through the OMB to ensure consistency with the president's policy.

145. (B) The spoils system ended with civil service reform in the 1880s. This reform ended the practice of patronage as rewards to the political faithful by party bosses so that civil servants were not removed due to the rotation of elected officials holding office. In their place, professional, career civil servants took over and created the first federal bureaucracies.

146. (C) The cabinet is the primary level of bureaucracy. These departments represent major policy sectors that require a large amount of attention due to their importance to the American government. The president's cabinet comprises positions for career civil servants who have specific expertise that can benefit the president and who can oversee their agency's performance.

147. (C) These departments grew out of the needs of American citizens and specific business groups, so the corresponding cabinet positions were added. The Defense, Treasury, and Justice departments provide a general need that apply to all citizens and the workings of government.

148. (B) With all of the military divisions under one umbrella, the Defense Department is the largest cabinet department and one of the country's biggest employers. It also has a budget in excess of $500 billion.

149. (C) The creation of the Department of Veterans Affairs was almost completely symbolic; it was a political gesture to those who had served in the military and was not an agency that required an increase in bureaucratic structure to make it function more efficiently.

150. (A) After the perceived weakness of coordinate national security information, the department of Homeland Security was created to centralize security data and better protect the country.

151. (C) Executive agencies do not fall under the auspices of any cabinet-level department and are therefore not under the oversight of congressional approval required for the holders of cabinet positions. This allows the president more room to place individuals loyal to his or her agenda who may not receive congressional approval.

152. (A) These agencies are controlled by Congress to make sure that proper oversight is given to industries. They are independent from executive control so that the president is not tempted to influence or tamper with regulations.

153. (D) These corporations are controlled by the government but differ from bureaucratic agencies because they operate like businesses. A prime example is the U.S. Postal Service. The service enjoys government connections, but it is run as a corporation, with the government position of postmaster general at the head of the organization.

154. (B) This method allows for the administration of bureaucratic policy to take place at a different government level or through private contractors. This can lead to political problems, such as the use of private security forces during the Iraq War. Private contractors worked alongside the military to secure strategic areas, protect American leaders, and provide military support when needed. Unfortunately, the military did not have oversight authority of these private companies that all too often pursued their own agendas in Iraq, which damaged American standing in the area and perhaps put American military forces in danger.

155. (B) Institutional autonomy is strong in the federal bureaucracy because the heads of these agencies, as well as the rank and file workers, have greater expertise in these areas and are usually left alone to go about their business and submit reports to government oversight organizations.

156. (B) Although the Senate must confirm appointments, the sheer number of bureaucratic appointments the president makes precludes intense Senate oversight except for controversial choices at the highest levels of the bureaucracy.

157. (D) In response to the Vietnam and Korean Wars, which were never declared wars, Congress sought to limit the commander in chief's ability to enter conflicts. The U.S. president must also be out of the conflict within 60 days, otherwise Congress can pull military funding. This law has proven to be ineffective, because once a president has committed troops, it is politically impossible to cut funding to the troops and put American lives at risk. Hence, we have the recent example of the Iraq War, where many in Congress disagreed with U.S. involvement, but they did not cut funding for the soldiers.

158. (D) The extreme size of the bureaucracy, plus the other responsibilities of the president, precludes such orders from being a legitimate option when trying to set the policy agenda. Working with interest groups is a more effective use of the president's time, and ultimately the president does not possess the authority to issue orders, even though bureaucrats often serve at the pleasure of the president.

159. (D) The bully pulpit possessed by the president is the easiest way for a party to get a message out. If the president is effective, the party benefits. If he or she is not, it suffers. The president, because of this position of authority, can help set the direction of the party in general, as was the case with Bill Clinton moving the Democrats closer to the ideological center in the 1990s.

160. (D) Executive orders have the power of law as long as they do not conflict with any existing legislation or the Constitution. Because the president can issue orders unilaterally, policy can change instantly.

161. (D) At the time of the New Deal, the federal government had been expanding its authority for most of the nation's history. The crisis of the Great Depression enabled

President Roosevelt to expand it at a quicker rate, but given the historical trend of increased national authority, it stands to reason that the federal government would have continued to grow as it still does today.

162. (B) The Great Society, which included Johnson's War on Poverty, was a social policy expansion that was akin to the regulatory expansion of the New Deal. This program created Medicare and Medicaid as well as increased the welfare programs in the states. It created huge federal spending and increased the federal mandates imposed on states.

163. (D) Although Congress does have final oversight, the bureaucracy was established long ago as part of the executive branch. Most policy functions are performed from the executive branch, of which the president is the head, so the president has great control over the policy agenda.

164. (A) Independent government corporations provide a means for an industry to be under government control but run like a business. The U.S. Postal Service is a government organization but runs its day-to-day operations like a separate corporation. Congress keeps the authority to constrain activities as needed but does not run the business.

165. (D) In the modern political arena, the president holds tremendous power to reach the American people and influence policy. Couple this ability with the agreement of the executives of important states, and national policy can change. If the president wants to start an initiative and receives support from states with large populations, then he or she will have the political means to change policy because public opinion will be in his or her favor.

166. (C) Congress provides ultimate approval to the actions and policies of the bureaucracy.

Chapter 5: The Judiciary and Policy Making

167. (A) According to Article I, section 8 in the Constitution, Congress has the power to regulate commerce between the states. Congress passed the Gun Control Act using the commerce clause as the constitutional power to do so. Although Congress had good intentions, the Court struck the law down because commerce was not legitimately being regulated here.

168. (C) The Supreme Court did not overturn many federal laws prior to the Civil War (*Dred Scott* was the only other case). *Marbury v. Madison* established that the court had judicial review over laws to ensure constitutionality. The case involved the refusal of the Jefferson administration to seat a federal judge given his seat through the Judiciary Act of 1801 in the waning days of the Adams administration. In striking down the act and denying Marbury his appointment, Chief Justice Marshall provided the legal basis for judicial review.

169. (B) This was the initial disagreement over the Constitution; the question of states' rights prevailed until the Civil War settled the issue. All other responses held little sway in the political mind-set of the day compared to the role of the states and the national government.

170. (B) The last enumerated power given to Congress, also known as the elastic clause, was interpreted in this case to provide Congress with the ability to create a national bank.

The power was not explicit, but the Supreme Court's interpretation of necessary and proper stated that Congress has discretion to create legislation it deems necessary.

171. (A) With the rise of the Industrial Revolution and the growth of corporations, there were many legal disputes between the government and private industry. During this time, the court was mostly proindustry and antigovernment intrusion and struck down laws aimed at aiding workers. Through these decisions, the Court established precedent for maintaining property rights of corporations against government intrusion.

172. (D) In perhaps his greatest political blunder, Roosevelt sought to reconstitute the court because he was angry at the justices for overturning key New Deal legislation. While he may have lost the political battle, he won the war, as over the next few years, four justices retired from the bench.

173. (D) The Supreme Court is the ultimate destination in a judge's career, and most will never reach it. However, the federal judiciary is relatively small, and not following precedent again and again will be noticed and can hurt a judge's hopes for career advancement. Further, any subsequent rulings will be given more scrutiny based on the judge's previous behavior.

174. (A) This is commonly called *judicial precedent* and determines future outcomes in legislation, policy, and court cases. Substantive doctrine is followed until it is overturned by a new precedent. The most recent precedent remains as doctrine.

175. (D) As government has become more complex, Congress and the president have instituted regulations and activities to deal with the complexity. With greater government activity comes more legal challenges, so it stands to reason that the Supreme Court has issued more decisions to interpret actions taken in a complex era of divided government.

176. (C) Placing a justice on the Supreme Court allows policy decisions to carry on long after presidents leave office. This sometimes backfires, as when a justice who does not subscribe to the ideology of the president who originally nominated him or her is placed on the Court. A legislative veto is an action that rejects the executive policy, while a Supreme Court appointment reinforces a cooperative effort by both elected branches.

177. (A) The Supreme Court may rule on a law, but Congress can pass laws that correct the problem found by the justices or reinforce the law despite the Court's finding.

178. (B) In theory, the Supreme Court has no enforcement authority for its decisions, and the other branches of government have ignored the Court from time to time. However, the American public views the Court as the legal authority; therefore, continued refusal by the elected branches to recognize the Court's decisions would erode electoral support.

179. (C) The Supreme Court is the referee and mediator between the legislative and executive branches and their struggle for power. The Court determines when legislation and executive action have crossed the constitutional line and keeps the other branches in check.

180. (C) The independence of the Court allows it to confront any government institution and protect infringement of rights and liberties, which may be abused or disregarded by the desires of some bureaucracies.

181. (B) This case involved President Harry Truman seizing the steel mills to avoid a strike by the workers. Truman took measures that went against existing legislation and believed he had the authority to do it. He felt that the mills needed to keep production moving because the United States was in the middle of the Korean War, and steel was of vital importance. The Supreme Court found that Truman did not have the authority to seize the mills to avoid a labor strike.

182. (C) While the manufacture of steel is important to the economy and any strike of a large industry will have negative effects, this case did not touch on the nation's debt.

183. (C) Rather than making rulings on the interpretation of the separation of powers in general, the Supreme Court has kept to a concise focus for review. It has limited its rulings to those cases involving private parties—be they individuals or corporations—or the government and raising the question of whether separation of powers was violated.

184. (A) Due to no set standard for separation of powers, the Supreme Court has actually maintained its credibility. The Court could have created a broad definition, through its power of judicial review, to severely inhibit the flexibility of the other branches. To its credit, it has refrained and, in doing so, kept its reputation as the arbiter of constitutional questions.

185. (B) The Supreme Court does not often make judgments on military or foreign relations activities as these involve quick-moving activities. Military engagements and incidents between nations do not often come to the Court's attention. If they do, they fall under the very narrow constitutional constructs of Article III, in which the Supreme Court has original jurisdiction—as with cases involving ambassadors and the like.

186. (A) Immigration represents a policy area where there is no clear distinction between elected branches of government. Bureaucracies, the president, and Congress all have some authority over different aspects of policymaking and agenda setting. Such gray areas call for detailed interpretation of the Constitution; thus cases pertaining to these issues are taken seriously by the Supreme Court, which attempts to clear up the matter through a decision if at all possible.

187. (B) The Constitution clearly separates legislative and executive powers. While modern bureaucracies may work more efficiently if they can straddle the two responsibilities, the Supreme Court will not allow violations of the Constitution.

188. (A) The more power a president is allowed to assume, the more the original intent of Article II is disregarded. Most government power is given to Congress, not the president. It may be easier in the modern age to streamline government processes through the executive branch, but that violates the Constitution; hence, the judicial restrictions placed on the president.

189. (B) Republican government is generally based on government representing the people but not intruding on their daily lives, as power is vested in elected representatives who pursue the interests of the governed. According to the Supreme Court, property rights were at the heart of that system until the New Deal expanded federal authority. Civil rights and government responsibility did not occupy the Court's time in the nineteenth century.

190. (D) The ultimate judicial decisions rest with Supreme Court rulings. These are the final interpretation of the Constitution as it applies to the laws and policies in question. The view can change, but usually there is a significant length of time before the Court changes view and creates a new precedent.

Chapter 6: Networking within the Federal Government

191. (C) Iron triangles are not usual because the three components rarely find common ground; however, they are extremely powerful when they do exist, because they control all aspects of the policymaking process.

192. (C) As noted in the preceding answer, iron triangles have no oversight, because the entities responsible for all three parts of policy formation—advocacy, organization, and implementation—work together.

193. (C) Once Congress or the public become aware of either entity or a cooperative effort, investigations are launched, and the relationship changes or new regulations are put into place. Public awareness is aroused because something bad happens as a result of the lack of oversight, as with the BP oil spill.

194. (C) The APA, passed in 1946, covers all rule making by government agencies. Since it was initially passed, court rulings have required even more stringent procedures in making and meeting rules required by the act.

195. (A) Red tape may be frustrating, but its existence demonstrates that the government agency in question has a set of procedures in place to meet requested action. The process may be laborious, depending on what agency and benefit are involved, but the process itself shows progress.

196. (C) Government action is slow and plodding, and bureaucracies reflect that. Efficiency is important, but in government and bureaucratic terms, efficiency cannot trump thorough processing and evaluation of activity. Further, government is interested in maintaining the status quo rather than bringing about quick change or an overhaul of existing systems.

197. (A) Divided government, where one party controls Congress and the other controls the presidency, has been a staple of modern American government. Legislative outcomes demonstrate little difference between this structure and a unified government, but it is perceived to cause more gridlock because the parties are at odds with each other.

198. (C) The elected branches may know what is permissible and the judiciary would seemingly agree. Every situation is unique, and the courts are reluctant to bind the activities of the other branches unless there is a clear violation of constitutional principles.

199. (A) To end a gridlock, every participant in the negotiations wants to get a concession or concessions. As this process unfolds, narrow constituencies win the day, because provisions that otherwise would not have been considered due to the small number desiring them are included to build a large enough coalition to move the action through the gridlock.

200. (A) Due to the compromises mentioned in the answer to question 445, consistent purpose cannot be maintained, and many irrelevant or unconnected aspects attach themselves to the action at hand.

201. (D) Congress and the president are usually at odds over policy goals, regardless of whether the government is unified or divided. However, when true policy disagreements occur, which side controls the action is of great importance. Through this struggle, the agency in question is torn between allegiance to the executive and requirements demanded by Congress.

202. (D) Although the bureaucracy implements the policy, it has little input on who controls the policy being made. Bureaucrats may be asked what their perspectives are, but they have no review process to determine the outcome of where control lies.

203. (C) Control authority ultimately rests with Congress as the legislative body. Institutionalizing the presidency limits executive control through legislative fiat and is therefore a limit placed before action takes place—an ex ante control.

204. (D) As issues have increased in number, so has the range of different perspectives that take positions on those issues. Rather than finding a general consensus or middle ground, extremism takes root, because extremists are often the loudest voices, if not the greatest number. This is particularly true in a highly partisan and polarized political atmosphere such as the one that currently exists.

205. (B) The polarization mentioned previously allowed George W. Bush to assume a large amount of policy control for the first six years of his presidency. The Republican majority in Congress raised little opposition, as the government was unified and there was little disagreement among party members as to the direction policy should follow.

206. (D) Of the organizations listed, only the Business Roundtable was directly created by government—in this case, the commerce secretary under Richard Nixon. NOW was formed from attendees of a government-sponsored conference on women's issues who were frustrated by how their government positions limited their actions. The NAACP and MADD formed due to a need for public awareness on the marginalization of African Americans and the dangers of drinking and driving, respectively. Government is often connected to or partially responsible for most interest groups, either through suggesting their creation or through legislative activity (or inactivity) that necessitates the creation of such groups.

207. (A) There is a general perception among the public that legislators draft legislation. However, due to the often-complex nature of formulating and organizing the myriad of details involved in creating legislation, interest group expertise is needed to help draft and often write large portions of legislation. The more interest groups are involved, the more complex the legislation. This is partly why legislation totaling more than 2,000 pages, such as the recent health care bill, is produced.

208. (A) In the 1990s, unified party control became suspect as political scientist David Mayhew analyzed the legislative effectiveness of unified government. He discovered that there was little legislative difference between times of unified government and times of divided government. Legislation was still passed in similar numbers and included the same amount of important legislation that affected the public.

209. (D) The performance of Congress—the legislation it produces in a given two-year term—can depend on a variety of factors including those given in this list. Public mood affects voter perception about candidates and parties. Congress is also affected by who is in the White House and broader policy concerns that may have far-reaching consequences.

210. (D) Woodrow Wilson, a political scientist himself, felt that the president could utilize both public opinion and party influence without being closely attached to either. His theory was to let these two forces work against each other to make both sides conform; parties forge opinion, and opinion forges party agendas with the president orchestrating the interaction.

211. (B) Cabinet posts are not nearly as powerful as they were before the New Deal, because the government has become highly complex. The complexity caused the need for a larger bureaucracy more directly under the influence of the president, which usurped the authority previously found in the cabinet.

212. (C) If a report on proposed legislation receives negative feedback from the populace, it is unlikely that the legislation will move forward. Elected officials want to remain in office, and this is done by keeping the voters happy. Negative or positive news affect the actions of elected officials.

213. (B) The media welcome basic government regulation of the industry to maintain an order and a structure as to how the industry operates. Of course, any infringement on freedom of the press would never be tolerated, but the news industry is a business like any other, and government regulation streamlines the organization and creates rules by which all must abide.

214. (A) The information the media delivers is most often provided by the government in the form of reports and analyses that break the issues down into salient parts. The news media do not have the resources or capability to perform this detailed research on their own, so they rely on government production for the data on which they build their stories.

215. (B) As the government grew and elected officials' responsibilities increased, they had less and less time to meet with reporters. Press secretaries provide the media with what they need and allow officials to conduct other business. This is most readily seen with the presidential press secretary, who meets with reporters daily to discuss the issues and the president's activities, something for which the modern president would not have time.

216. (D) The bureaucracy contains experts in the fields that they oversee, and most decisions are left to their discretion. Only when there is a policy change or they have come under oversight from Congress are decisions made elsewhere in government. The day-to-day operation of policy is left in the hands of bureaucrats.

217. (B) The formula factors in variables based on population, region, and so on are relatively clear, and no area gets more than its fair share. However, trade-offs are necessary when creating these formulas, as everyone cannot receive everything they want. So everyone gets something, but nobody gets everything.

218. (B) Earmarks require no trade-offs because they are one-off programs or projects that are usually attached to a larger bill and benefit one or a few elected officials. The programs or projects are usually regional and offer the elected official(s) receiving the earmark the ability to go back to his or her constituents and let them know what he or she got for them.

219. (B) Congress is ultimately a collection of regional interests. If an interest group wants to lobby effectively, a good method is to utilize the parochialism inherent in the system to the group's advantage.

220. (D) As policymaking rests firmly with bureaucracies, so does the creation of the agenda. Unless there is a reason for Congress to do otherwise, it will defer to agency expertise as to the best way of moving forward in developing and implementing policy.

221. (C) Delegation allows the bureaucracy to handle details, while Congress and the president take care of larger political and policy goals. Delegation allows for everyone's needs, including the public's, to be met consistently.

222. (A) Political turnover is a fact of the American political system. Those in power leave or lose elections or move to other offices. Thus, bureaucratic leadership and direction may change with new presidential administrations or a new party in control of Congress.

223. (B) Bureaucracies are made up of people with opinions and perspectives on the best way to accomplish a goal. Due to their expertise, they are often deferred to by those with control of the policy apparatus. Couple this with the complexity of information and situations arise in which Congress may not receive what it thinks is relevant because the agency representatives do not think it is relevant, or they would rather not share it because it may alter their policy implementations.

224. (C) Like any network, these are the players who push policy forward. Interest groups, politicians, and bureaucratic agencies comprise these networks and include just about everyone involved in government at one time or another depending on the issue.

225. (C) The policy question at hand is clarified and streamlined for public understanding and consumption. Points are highlighted so that voters can take an educated stand on the issue and the ensuing policy represents the efforts of all parts of the policy network.

226. (D) Government officials are part of the policy networks, but all other participants help inform them of the latest information. Lobbying by the interest groups is coupled with bureaucratic analysis to provide the elected official with everything he or she needs to know to make decisions and act on policy initiatives.

227. (B) This goes back to the cost-benefit analysis that politicians must make. Policy networks provide the means to help politicians answer the question, is it worth it?

228. (A) It is sometimes easier to challenge a policy in court than it is to go through the process of changing the legislation. The judiciary plays a role outside the policy network, validating the network's efforts by deciding in its favor.

PART 3 CIVIL LIBERTIES AND CIVIL RIGHTS

Chapter 7: Civil Liberties: Incorporation of the 14th Amendment

229. (A) The latest incorporation case, the ruling in *McDonald* acknowledged the right to possess a gun extended to the states as well as the federal government. After *McDonald*, state gun control laws came under great scrutiny.

230. (A) This case involved eminent domain in the Fifth Amendment. A shipping company was affected by the actions of the city of Baltimore when the city dumped sand and earth from a road construction project around the wharf, making the water too shallow for ships to use. The company was no longer able to conduct business and sought compensation from the city of Baltimore under eminent domain, which states that government needs to provide compensation for the loss or taking of any property for the public good. The Court found that eminent domain only applied to the federal government and not state action, and Baltimore was not required to compensate the company.

231. (C) Freedom of speech is in the Bill of Rights and, until the twentieth century, did not apply to state action. *Gitlow v. New York* did apply freedom of speech to state action, as it prohibited states from limiting the speech of their residents.

232. (B) The incorporation doctrine, which extends the Bill of Rights, is made possible by the Fourteenth Amendment. This was a pivotal shift in the Supreme Court's reasoning and has allowed the expansion of rights and liberties to extend to citizens through every level of government.

233. (D) Due process is the procedure the government uses in its dealings with citizens. There is a due process clause in the Fifth Amendment, but that was traditionally believed to apply only to federal government action. The incorporation doctrine of the Fourteenth Amendment applied due process to all levels of government.

234. (A) The Supreme Court has reasoned that law enforcement on the local level must meet the needs of the community and region. Constitutional rights must be provided, but every practice of local law enforcement does not necessarily require close constitutional scrutiny, nor is it necessarily a violation of Fourteenth Amendment due process.

235. (B) These Bill of Rights amendments are included in states' rights through the incorporation doctrine. Only the grand jury provision of the Fifth Amendment has not been applied. The Third Amendment has never been ruled on by the Supreme Court, and the Seventh Amendment does not apply.

Chapter 8: Civil Liberties: 1st, 2nd, & 4th Amendments

236. (D) Using the First Amendment's establishment clause, the *Engel* case struck down the state of New York's attempt to start the public school day with a prayer. The Court ruled the prayer violated the constitutional concept of "separation of church and state" when the state established a statewide prayer.

237. (A) In this Vietnam War era case, the *N.Y. Times* printed a leaked article from the Pentagon. The Nixon White House attempted to suppress the article using prior restraint. The Supreme Court ruled against the federal government allowing the media some latitude in what is published.

238. (B) The *Schenck* case created the famous "clear and present danger test," which means if speech causes a immediate danger for fellow citizens that speech is not protected. A famous limitation on free speech, Justice Oliver Wendell Holmes used the famous example: "You can't yell fire in a crowded theater."

239. (B) Like many states, Wisconsin created a compulsory school attendance law until the age of 16. Amish in that state contended the law violated the religious sect's right to free exercise of religion because that level of education was not needed in their society. The Court agreed and dropped the Amish compulsory education to the eighth grade.

240. (D) Although students rights to free speech are limited in schools, the *Tinker* case stated that a student's right to free speech "does not end at the schoolhouse gate." Wearing black armbands to protest the Vietnam War, John and MaryBeth challenged the school suspension and won.

241. (B) The terms are often grouped together, but the distinction between them is that people either have a right *to* something or are free *from* something.

242. (B) Supreme Court judges and justices have personal ideologies that determine what cases they will choose to hear and how they will rule. Advocates try to determine the prevailing attitude of the Court to see whether they have a chance of winning a favorable decision.

243. (D) The culture of today is more accepting of different groups and practices than ever before. The substance of legislation is interpreted in the context of this culture, so the more liberal the culture is, the more accepting of diversity and various practices legislation will be.

244. (C) This case is important legal doctrine because it establishes a limit to what most Americans view as their most fundamental right—freedom of speech. The Supreme Court found that speech that incites violence or panic is not permissible, with Justice Oliver Wendell Holmes making the analogy that someone cannot yell fire in a crowded movie theater because that might lead to injury.

245. (A) This has proven true since the terrorist attacks on September 11, 2001. Historically, the government is empowered to curtail rights and liberties in times of crisis by citizens who value immediate protection over constitutional protection. This does not justify the laws and policies that limit civil rights, but politicians are empowered because the immediate public demand is for protection, not freedom.

246. (C) In *Dennis v. United States*, the clear and present danger test, which implies an immediate threat to safety, was extended to include the possibility of danger in the future.

This affects speech much more, as the interpretation is broad enough to limit a wide range of speech that threatens the status quo. Not surprisingly, this ruling was made during the Red Scare of the 1940s and 1950s, when Americans were concerned about the threat of communism. The Supreme Court decision reflects the social attitudes of the time.

247. (B) Obscenity has been an issue in free speech cases, because it is hard to define. *Roth v. United States* offered little help in interpretation, as it called for applying "contemporary community standards" to see if something was obscene. Who decides what the standards are was not discussed.

248. (C) Another obscenity case, this ruling argued that there can be no national standard and that state and local governments are the best arbiters of obscenity because they are closest to the local population. This is not a truly viable option, as different regions have different cultures; therefore, some citizens may enjoy freedoms that others are denied. Laws across the country still reflect local cultural and social preferences, limiting activities on certain days and applying curfews to curb certain undesirable behavior.

249. (A) This question is about what right the press has to find out and publish the name of a person accused of a crime. For example, the criminal justice system is based on the theory of people being innocent until proven guilty. However, it is hard to receive a fair trial if news reports claim you murdered someone. This is a struggle between two fundamental rights within the Bill of Rights itself. As with speech, there are limits to what the press is free to do, and legislation can be passed that reasonably limits the press in order to protect the innocent.

250. (C) The government cannot establish one religion or give one religion any better legal standing than another. This has been generally interpreted with the free exercise clause as granting freedom of religion.

251. (B) Laws that impact religion are immediately suspect as limiting the practice of religion or favoring one religion over another. However, that does not mean that laws touching on religious issues are automatically disqualified. The Supreme Court looks at the intent of the law to determine whether there is a secular legislative purpose to it, such as charity contributions or services that do not endorse any religion.

252. (D) In *Lemon v. Kurtzman*, the Supreme Court attempted to create a test that determined whether a law violated the establishment clause. The *Lemon* test, as it came to be known, consisted of three parts: the statute in question must have a secular legislative purpose; its primary effect must be one that neither advances nor inhibits religion; and it must not foster an excessive government entanglement with religion. The confusion in subsequent decisions made the *Lemon* test fade from use; it was replaced with the question of whether the law remained neutral in its approach.

253. (D) *Engel v. Vitale*, still decried in conservative circles nearly 50 years later, banned prayer in public schools, which was found to be a violation of church and state. Because schools were publicly funded entities, prayer in schools was a government endorsement of religion and thus violated the establishment clause.

254. (D) The other protection not listed is freedom to petition the government for a redress of grievances. All citizens can seek to change laws they feel are unjustified, and they will not be punished in any way by the government for issuing their complaints. The Founding Fathers believed this to be as important to a free society as the other guarantees in the First Amendment.

255. (B) The Fourth Amendment is the first in the Bill of Rights that applies to the criminally accused. Government needs a legitimate reason to search a person's private belongings for evidence of wrongdoing. This prevents the government from choosing to harass citizens for reasons that would be considered discriminatory or biased in any way.

256. (D) These two cases were pivotal in framing the right to privacy. Both deal with the personal choices that a woman makes regarding her own body—either to prevent pregnancy through the use of contraception or to terminate an unwanted pregnancy through abortion. The latter has had political ramifications ever since the ruling due to the fact that many people believe abortion is legalized murder because life begins at conception.

257. (D) The Ninth Amendment states that any powers not given to Congress are reserved for the people. Thus, because there is no right to privacy in the Constitution, it is not associated with Congress and must belong to the people. The Supreme Court has used this amendment sparingly in deciding privacy cases.

258. (D) The right to privacy, the basis of *Roe*, was recognized in *Griswold v. Connecticut*. A penumbra officially created by *Griswold*, the right to privacy became the foundation for the right to abortion found in *Roe*.

Chapter 9: Civil Liberties: Procedural Due Process

259. (C) An incorporation case, *Gideon* recognized the right to an attorney in where most criminal cases take place—in the state courts. After *Gideon* public defenders were installed throughout the United States and true justice was served.

260. (C) The Fourth, Fifth, Sixth, and Eighth Amendments mirror the legal progression of the criminally accused. The Fourth Amendment protects against illegal searches and seizures. The Fifth Amendment prevents self-incrimination, gives the accused the right to a grand jury trial, prohibits double jeopardy, and guarantees due process. The Sixth Amendment requires a quick and speedy trial in front of a jury of one's peers, as well as the right to an attorney. Finally, the Eighth Amendment prevents cruel and unusual punishment by the government or the setting of excessive bail.

261. (C) *Mapp v. Ohio* extended Fourth Amendment protections to the states. It found that evidence obtained in violation of the Fourth Amendment's illegal search and seizure requirements must be excluded from state criminal proceedings.

262. (A) This is the case that requires the police to read suspects their rights. As seen in every television and movie depiction of an arrest since 1966, when someone is placed under arrest, the officers say, "You have the right to remain silent . . ."—which is a reading of the accused's Fifth and Sixth Amendment rights.

263. (B) The British government detained colonists for crimes and threatened to send them back to England to stand trial. Fearful that, left unchecked, the new American government might eventually try similar tactics, the Anti-Federalists pushed for protections for those standing trial in a criminal case.

264. (B) The plaintiff in *Gideon v. Wainwright* was an indigent transient accused of breaking into a pool hall. At trial, he could not afford a lawyer, and the judge refused to provide him with one. Once convicted, he studied the law and appealed his conviction on constitutional grounds. His case demonstrates that the American judicial system can correct any wrong and that any citizen can receive justice if the law is on his or her side.

265. (D) The case found that arbitrary sentencing of capital punishment was cruel and unusual punishment, violating the Eighth Amendment. It did not say the death penalty itself was unconstitutional; rather, the inconsistency of state statutes regarding sentencing was wrong. States rewrote the statutes, and Georgia's rewrite became a model followed by other states; the death penalty was reinstated four years later.

266. (D) Criminal rights for those accused of state crimes are relatively recent in American judicial history because of the confusion of what rights applied and the sentiment of the general public, which believed in harsh punishment for criminals.

267. (A) Penumbras are the "shadows" of the Constitution, where intent can be implied or inferred. Such is the case for the right to privacy. Most Americans agree that everyone has a right to privacy; however, nowhere in the Constitution is such a right defined. Through the interpretation of the penumbras in existing constitutional amendments and provisions, the Supreme Court has created and shaped such a right.

268. (C) This recent case is controversial because it is a new interpretation of eminent domain. Historically, the Supreme Court has permitted the government to purchase property at market value to provide a service that benefits society, such as building a hospital or roads that everyone can use. *Kelo* held that a city can force the purchase of property in a blighted area to bring economic redevelopment to that area. Critics of this ruling fear that it may open the door for cities to clear out rundown, poorer neighborhoods to bring in gentrification projects. The lower classes would be displaced, regardless of whether they were paid for their property.

Chapter 10: Civil Rights: Equal Protection Under the Law

269. (A) Equal protection under the law is something that continues to be interpreted by the Supreme Court. From the civil rights movement of the 1950s and 1960s to gender equality today, the Court uses equal protection as a measure to ensure that all citizens enjoy the same rights. There are still classes and groups of people fighting for their rights, and equal protection will most likely be the argument they use.

270. (C) Although passed in 1867, the Fourteenth Amendment's due process clause was not fully realized until the mid-twentieth century through federal litigation. In *Brown* the Supreme Court struck down the ability of states to segregate based on race and overturned *Plessy v. Ferguson.*

271. (C) Legislation designed to limit activity or deny a group the opportunity to do what others are allowed to do is suspect. This does not mean that the group is suspicious, rather it refers to the historic discrimination or marginalization the group has faced in society and through legal limitations.

272. (D) The strict scrutiny given fundamental rights in landmark civil rights cases in the 1950s and 1960s looked at how individuals and groups were treated by the law in terms of restrictions and discrimination in the legal process. All the responses reflect those considerations.

273. (D) This question refers to the transition from Chief Justice Earl Warren to Chief Justice Warren Burger in 1969. The two-tier approach was one between the "old," or flexible, interpretation of equal protection and the Warren Court's "new" strict interpretation. The clause in question is the equal protection clause of the Fourteenth Amendment, which had been developed under the strict scrutiny to be used by the Court as an intervention to thwart legislative action that violated the clause. Many thought there would be a shift away from civil rights with Burger's appointment, but the new chief justice did not drive the Court away from the precedents set under Warren.

274. (A) Voting and ballot access were viewed as fundamental to the rights of citizens, and any legislation, whether state or federal, designed to limit that access was struck down by the Supreme Court.

275. (D) The deferential approach refers to the traditional way the Supreme Court viewed equal protection, granting leeway to legislation and trying to determine its intent. The Court does not necessarily overturn legislation when using this type of scrutiny.

276. (B) This refers to the famous *Dred Scott* decision that held that slaves were not people and therefore had no legal standing to sue for their freedom. This is considered to be the worst Supreme Court ruling in history due to its absurd premise that slaves were not people.

277. (C) Reconstruction allowed Republicans to control the South and provide newly freed slaves a way to participate in government. If the South were allowed to come back unassisted, it would automatically increase its representation in the House because former slaves would count as part of the population. Fearing a loss of power, the controlling Republican Party instituted Reconstruction, in part, to guarantee electoral victory.

278. (A) *Plessy v. Ferguson* resulted in a decision that validated Jim Crow laws in the South at the end of the nineteenth century. Plessy, who was one-eighth African American, was arrested for riding in a whites-only passenger car on a train. The Supreme Court held that as long as alternative accommodations were made, separate but equal was constitutional.

279. (C) *Brown v. Board of Education of Topeka* was the landmark case that desegregated schools and represents how the Supreme Court can overturn its own precedents. The Court reasoned that separate facilities are inherently unequal based on the fact that they are separate. It was some time before desegregation was complete, but *Brown* began the process through its ruling.

280. (C) Affirmative action, designed to level the playing field for groups that were historically discriminated against, was applied to many different situations, including college and graduate school admissions. Often, schools would set quotas to satisfy the need for diversity. This case stated that such quotas were unconstitutional because it amounted to reverse discrimination in limiting the opportunity of people based on the color of their skin.

281. (D) Although not true for most of this country's history, the civil rights struggles of African Americans helped usher in an era in which basic rights and liberties are protected for all Americans. This does not mean that all groups enjoy the same freedoms, but the established doctrine points to favoring individual rights and freedoms.

282. (B) Article I, section 8's commerce clause has become controversial because Congress has used this power in a variety of ways, like passing civil rights legislation. Although well intentioned, the Supreme Court struck down the federal gun restriction because the law didn't regulate commerce at all, thus going beyond Congressional constitutional powers.

283. (C) *Lawrence v. Texas* overturned an earlier Supreme Court ruling that upheld antisodomy laws. In overturning the previous ruling, the Court cited an individual's right to privacy protections.

284. (D) Some feel that this act interferes too much with the function of small business, while others believe that it does not cover all those who should be protected under the law. Because states interpret it differently and the courts have not issued consistent rulings, administration of the law will continue to be incomplete, creating more legal action by people seeking remedies.

285. (A) A strong national majority is needed to change social behaviors and legislative action. Judicial rulings are a large part of establishing the correct position, but the public, through their elected officials, must demand change for it to fully take effect.

286. (D) Liberties are threatened when they limit the behaviors of individuals and groups. The Constitution does not make a distinction that if a majority of the public disapproves of an activity, that majority has the right to prevent the activity. On the contrary, the Supreme Court has reasoned that such liberties are vital to the continued function of society, as social preferences cannot be legislated.

287. (B) This amendment has been used to apply the protections of the Bill of Rights, designed to limit the power of the federal government, to state governments.

288. (D) Reconstruction was the organized method of returning former Confederate states to the Union by guaranteeing the civil and legal rights of former slaves. The Fourteenth

Amendment grants citizenship and all the rights that entails to all former slaves. The due process and equal protection clauses have been used to guarantee citizenship rights to many other groups since.

289. (A) Initially, the Supreme Court took a direct interpretation of the equal protection clause. If Congress or a state legislature passed a law, it had a legislative purpose to do so. The violation would have to be readily apparent to be struck down, and the benefit of the doubt went to the government in creating necessary laws.

290. (C) Earl Warren's tenure as chief justice saw sweeping changes in the perspective of the Supreme Court's interpretation of equal protection. This interpretation led to several landmark cases that brought civil rights and liberties to residents who suffered discrimination under state government action and policy.

291. (D) The 1873 case involved a suit over New Orleans granting a monopoly to one slaughterhouse company as a violation of the due process and privileges and immunities clauses of the Fourteenth Amendment. The Supreme Court found that broad application of the Fourteenth Amendment would degrade state governments by subjecting them to the control of Congress.

292. (A) Originally, as part of Reconstruction, the Fourteenth Amendment granted citizenship and guaranteed rights to former slaves in order to prevent the anticipated racial discrimination they would face. When Reconstruction failed after 12 years, the era of Jim Crow and segregation ensued.

293. (B) In a series of Supreme Court cases, including *Brown v. Board of Education*, the NAACP repeatedly made the due process and equal protection arguments. Once the rulings were established, state-sponsored segregation and discrimination were struck down, and laws at all levels of government represented this new legal understanding and interpretation.

294. (D) A suspect classification refers to a group that has suffered organized discrimination in the past. Gender has only recently been seen as a possible suspect class, although not to the same extent as minority groups. However, the Supreme Court has become more open to the possibility, perhaps because women are now Supreme Court judges.

295. (A) This case involved the internment of Japanese American citizens during World War II. The military issued orders to detain Japanese citizens due to a possible attack by the Japanese on the West Coast. The Supreme Court found that even though strict scrutiny was used, the military still had a responsibility to protect all citizens, even if it meant sacrificing the rights of a few. Further, the court reasoned that because it was not possible to separate the loyal Japanese from the disloyal, the military was reasonable in removing all Japanese Americans.

296. (D) Gender has not been placed on the same level of classification as race, but the Supreme Court has come to recognize that gender may be something of a suspect class and that a heightened level of scrutiny is required in cases that demonstrate gender discrimination.

297. (B) Although most students are familiar with *Brown v. the Board* (1954), or *Brown I*, the Court gave power to federal district courts to oversee desegregation through *Brown II*, decided in 1955. That case decided desegregation should take place "with all deliberate speed."

298. (A) The Supreme Court has rejected the contention that the mentally ill have historically suffered discrimination. The Court did not state what level should be used in determining whether the rights of the mentally ill have been denied, but it did not find that they were a suspect class of any kind.

299. (C) Some opponents to the ERA argued that the amendment was extraneous. Proper interpretation of the Fourteenth Amendment's equal protection clause could provide relief to distressed groups, such as women. Proponents of the amendment argue that women need more focused and directed constitutional protection.

300. (C) The Supreme Court requires proof of purposeful discrimination in the content or administration of the law. This includes laws that are facially neutral. The controversy over this standard is that it is unclear what data should be used to make a determination of purposeful discrimination.

301. (D) The ruling for the desegregation of schools was a pivotal moment in the civil rights movement; however, implementing it was more difficult. The Supreme Court extended the Fourteenth Amendment to apply to the achievement of a certain result. This brought the court to reason that equal protection required not only that desegregation end but that proper implementation take place. This was in response to the South's slow progress in desegregating schools.

302. (B) The Fourteenth Amendment provides that every person born or naturalized in the United States is a U.S. citizen. Recently, as the political debate over immigration has increased, some people have called for this part of the amendment to be revised to prevent "anchor babies." Immigrants, often illegal, come to this country to give birth. The child would automatically be an American citizen, and the parents would be allowed to stay. A decision that was originally meant to grant full citizenship to freed slaves has grown to include anyone born on American soil.

303. (D) The Supreme Court has substantiated, through case law, the fundamental interest in voting and the electoral process. Any law that infringes on, affects, or denies this interest is struck down as a violation of equal protection. The law must show the highest scrutiny to justify any infringement, and the court rarely finds any legitimate justification when it comes to the limitation of voting rights or access to the electoral process.

304. (D) The business of government has become more involved in the private sector, merging the two interests. Therefore, all the responses apply to this situation. The Supreme Court has placed restraints on the private sector that are similar to those it has placed on government action.

305. (B) The Supreme Court has ruled that certain attempts to create new congressional districts to reflect a correction of past racial discrimination is unconstitutional and violates the equal protection clause. Additionally, any plan that dilutes an ethnicity or a race is prohibited.

306. (D) The amendment was created to end racial discrimination in the southern states. As Reconstruction failed, African Americans were relegated to second-class status once again. Jim Crow laws helped perpetuate segregation, and it was not until the 1950s that the Fourteenth Amendment became widely used to ensure rights for everyone.

307. (C) The Supreme Court has ruled that, although Congress has the ability to correct government and public action to ensure compliance with the amendment, Congress can also make sure that private entities in violation of the Fourteenth Amendment come into line. This greatly expands the power of the provisions, as they are more likely to be followed due to Congress's reach and authority.

308. (A) The rationality requirement sought to determine whether there was a minimal fit between classifications and objectives. Legislatures usually classify to some degree because statutes do not encompass all parts of society. Legislation has direction and purpose, and thus classification occurs. Equal protection demands that there be some rational connection to means and ends; otherwise, the constitutional standard is not met.

309. (A) After the passage of the Voter's Rights of 1965, states could apportion based on a state's racial demographics. Shaw reaffirmed that but stated this reapportionment was subject to close examination by the courts.

PART 4 AMERICAN POLITICAL IDEOLOGIES AND BELIEFS

Chapter 11: Political Socialization and Ideology

310. (C) Most citizens would like the government to do more for them, as long as they do not have to pay for it through higher taxes. This is the contradiction in today's society. Ever since the economic troubles of 2008, people have been steadfastly against raising taxes, but they want to hold on to expensive programs such as Medicare. As costs skyrocket, such actions are becoming untenable, creating an ideological rift between the major parties.

311. (D) The bedrock of this nation is personal liberty. Society recognizes, better than ever, when a group or a right is being discriminated against or infringed on. While most may not agree with certain lifestyles or practices, few truly want the government to officially sanction such lifestyles or practices.

312. (D) Although all the events above had huge impacts in our history, the Vietnam War and Watergate fueled a deep mistrust in our government and led to federal campaign finance laws, ended the military draft, and the resignation of a president.

313. (A) Recent research has shown the decline of political parties, the rise of interest groups, and most distrust in government, has led to more Americans identify as moderates and considered to be pivotal in presidential elections.

314. (D) Perhaps the most controversial decision of the twenty-first century, *Citizens United* reaffirmed the *Buckley* case and political donations were a form of political, thus free, speech. *Citizens United* also helped create "Super Pacs," PACS that could raise and spend unlimited amounts of money.

315. (B) There is little evidence to suggest that the average voter is better informed than in the past. While there may be more information available, that does not translate to more knowledge. In fact, the deluge of information could be a detriment to voter knowledge, as it is too much to process on one's own, and more and more people turn to opinion leaders to find out what is happening.

316. (D) Like most of our personality, it develops from the cues we pick up from our environment as we mature.

317. (A) Because we are most influenced by our surroundings, political socialization takes place as we grow up and listen to family and friends discuss their perspectives on political and social issues.

318. (D) Most studies have shown that educated and older people are the most reliable voting blocs. Young people are not reliable voters and tend to gravitate toward voting as they get older although voting in the United States is low overall when compared to other Western democracies.

319. (C) Other factors may influence certain individuals, but across society, the news media provide the information and messages voters see. This obviously places a burden on the media to cover all relevant information. Claims of bias in the media stem, in part, from the media being the primary source of political information.

320. (A) Ideologies are formed from a set of attitudes to help citizens identify their political standing. This includes labels such as *liberal* or *conservative*, where views on many issues may be bundled together to position oneself on the political spectrum.

321. (A) Conservatives believe that too much government interference is harmful to society and that individuals should be free to act in their own best interests with as little government input as possible, as long as no one gets hurt. Liberals believe that the role of government is to provide services and help citizens. Both groups also differ on social issues, with liberals believing government should stay out of people's business and conservatives generally holding the opposite view.

322. (C) Everyone has a set of beliefs that they hold dear and that shapes their attitudes as much as any other factor. If an ideology conflicts with their values, the core value will usually prevail. For example, someone may be generally liberal but be pro-life, even though the liberal ideology is pro-choice.

323. (C) To be partisan is to identify strongly with a political party and synthesize your values with those of that party. This pertains to all political parties, but in America's predominating two-party system, this usually means someone is a Democrat or a Republican.

324. (B) It is human nature to drift toward that with which we agree and move away from that with which we disagree. Therefore, political attitudes are not a neutral measurement but often show a high degree of bias, because individuals are going to find information that supports their belief structure rather than refutes it.

325. (B) Most people do not experience all major political issues. Some may lose jobs or suffer some sort of government intrusion, while others will decide to have or not have abortions. Regardless, people still hold views on a variety of issues because politics is the collective action of society for the collective good. Opinions reflect this fact.

326. (A) In the early years of the republic political parties controlled newspapers, sought out voters and informed them, and at times provided tangible rewards for voting for a party's candidate. With the rise of the electronic media, Americans became less reliant on parties for information.

327. (D) Those with high incomes tend to be better educated and therefore have had the opportunity to study, observe, and learn about different contributing factors surrounding social issues. This more nuanced view often leads to an understanding of conflicting viewpoints, and education encourages keeping a more open mind about social issues.

328. (B) The Eighteenth Amendment. Prohibition was largely the result of vigilant and organized anti-alcohol interest groups in the early twentieth century. Although these groups got their wish Prohibition is largely seen as a failure and repealed by the Twenty-First Amendment.

329. (C) The most prevailing political factor for many minorities in this country is the history of discrimination they have faced. Obviously, the history of African Americans is the prime example of how discrimination has affected a group's political participation, and that history continues to play a part in the formation of the group's political perspective.

Chapter 12: Public Opinion and Polling

330. (A) The other polls listed above are used to recognize political trends and gather information, while exit polls are used to monitor elections and help make predictions.

331. (C) As noted earlier, the media deliver the information, but in doing so, they must decide what news is. This necessary editorializing indirectly sets the political agenda because it determines what the public is made aware of and what politicians react to.

332. (C) Although all of the items above are more prevalent than in years past, voting by far is the way most Americans participate in the political process.

333. (C) Due to the lack of time most people have to learn, understand, and formulate political ideas, opinion leaders are used as cognitive shortcuts. These shortcuts allow voters to associate a belief structure with someone who has, in the past, seemed to represent wholly or partially that voter's general viewpoint. Thus, there is no need to conduct further research if the opinion leader has already provided a position on the issue.

334. (C) Aggregate public opinion becomes more consistent over time. This is due in large part to the consistent message of opinion leaders. As people coalesce around certain ideologies, general views will remain consistent.

335. (A) Public opinion's power is that it is the lifeblood of politics. If elected officials do not listen to what the public wants, they will lose their positions. This is not to say that politicians need to act only to please the public, but they need the skill to address the public's concerns and redirect opinion when necessary, so it appears that they are performing services their constituents desire.

336. (B) Scientific polling is statistical analysis of a random sampling of the population that allows politicians to discover what is on the collective mind of the American public. Once they understand this, public relations comes into play, shaping a consistent message for the individual politician or candidate that makes it appear that public concerns are being addressed. These two devices help the politician serve his or her constituency.

337. (B) Political attitude encompasses an individual's leaning toward political facts and provides a foundation for political ideology. Attitudes tend to be closer to an issue-by-issue perspective and constitute a set of generally held beliefs.

338. (D) Policy needs to reflect public opinion preference and must therefore take such preferences into consideration. This is not to say that policy is made at the whim of the public, but strong support or opposition to a policy will have an effect on that policy.

339. (B) More than any other social or moral issue, abortion has dominated political discussion for nearly four decades. Since abortion become legal with the ruling in *Roe v. Wade*, proponents for and against have been steadfast in their lobbying of politicians. Congress, the president, and the Supreme Court have had to address the issue, and candidates and judicial nominees alike must provide their views on it due to public demand.

340. (B) The Cold War between the United States and the Soviet Union created a bipolar world with two superpowers facing off. This simplified the international landscape for most citizens, and public opinion reflected that. In the years following the war's end in 1991, many variables have caused public opinion to vary from situation to situation. Terrorism, the trouble in the Middle East, and the rise of China's power have all contributed to a slightly wider worldview within public opinion.

341. (D) When taken as a whole, public opinion shows general, easily predictable trends. Individual responses may vary widely, but when all responses are combined, a definite consensus of thought forms that can be used to represent public opinion on the issue or issues politicians care (or should care) about.

Chapter 13: Linkage Institutions and Public Perception

342. (A) Politicians always want their actions placed in a positive perspective, but the news media look for the facts and information that are often detrimental to a politician's goals. This creates a natural conflict between the two groups.

343. (D) Politicians can sometimes ignore or overlook another politician's position on an issue. However, if they are called out in the media, they most certainly respond, because the public is made aware of the issue.

344. (B) If a politician wants to see whether an idea is acceptable, he or she floats it and sees if it flies, hence the analogy of the balloon.

345. (C) News leaks have the power to cause the media to investigate further and also make politicians respond to allegations or information they wish had not been made public.

346. (B) Due to the sheer size of government, news agencies cannot cover all government activity. However, if something of importance comes up in an area that does not have a beat reporter, an agency promptly reshuffle its staff to cover the story.

347. (C) Controversial and negative stories tend to attract more attention from the public and therefore bring more of a following to the news media. This trend is criticized by politicians and the public alike, but few make any effort to change the system.

348. (A) Each side wants to use the other for its own gain, and therefore, each side is territorial as to what its role is. Politicians want the media to treat them favorably, while the media want politicians to provide them with pertinent information.

349. (C) When a political scandal or cover-up happens, there is distrust between the media and elected officials. The media feel that the politicians have betrayed their relationship, and politicians feel that the media are only looking to end their political careers. Communication breaks down, and neither side wishes to work with the other in the same way. This separation creates a credibility gap, as the media demonstrate the malfeasance of the elected officials, and the elected officials choose not to address the media so the problem is not exacerbated.

350. (A) In pluralist systems, adamant minorities often defeat apathetic majorities. Therefore, the public sees little progress on issues, while there has been significant success in stopping legislation one side felt was harmful or against its political advantage. The public might not appreciate or like this fact, but it cannot legitimately be argued that nothing gets done.

351. (D) Being a member of Congress is demanding on several fronts. Politicians must be able to persuade, legislate, and oversee, and be knowledgeable about many government-related topics. Usually they do this while remaining generally anonymous to the public at large, except for astute political observers.

352. (D) Voter preference has much to do with electoral outcomes but little with how the parties act toward each other. Each party enjoys a loyal number of faithful members, but voters still decide what is best for themselves, and if a party has demonstrated it may be able to help them more, voters will turn out for that party's candidates at the polls.

353. (D) Interest groups are perhaps the best indicators elected officials have to gauge public opinion and determine whether a policy would be well received. Of course, there may be interest groups for both sides of an issue, so an official must work through opposing views, but he or she will still have a better understanding about public sentiment.

354. (B) Competing interest groups can lead to inaction, but gridlock requires compromise to be overcome. While elements of this compromise may not be relevant to the issue, there will be incremental progress on which to build. The complaints about gridlock are correct but only part of the entire process of how government gets things done.

355. (B) Interest groups have been around to advocate for certain sectors of society since the time this country was founded. The public interest lobby of the eighteenth century appealed to the public for support of those outside the established power structure with different goals from groups maintaining the status quo. Interest groups have developed with the government ever since.

356. (A) As noted earlier, growing complexity creates new interest groups that create even more complexity. It appears to be a somewhat self-perpetuating system.

357. (B) The narrow focus of industrial interest groups provides elected officials with a clear policy direction. The focus of social issues can vary from issue to issue, and many things may need to be provided. The lack of organization as well as strategic policy put marginalized groups further down on most elected officials' priority lists.

358. (C) Social movements—if they capture the public's attention—can garner significant political support, because no politician wants to be caught on the wrong side of an issue. However, this does not mean that elected officials immediately side with a movement as their constituents may not agree with it.

359. (C) Media saturation is a problem for Congress because the news media do not cover all issues, but often only a few issues in great detail. This prevents public awareness and understanding on the issues Congress faces. For example, any coverage on the budget may highlight tax increases or tax cuts and changes to popular, well-known programs, but it may overlook all the other necessary items that also must be considered. Conversely, the media may focus on one subsidy or provision that seems to give a disproportionate benefit to a small group and use that to represent wasteful spending. Without being able to cover the whole issue, Congress must address public concern and alter its legislative priorities.

360. (A) As noted earlier, each side needs the other, so it is to their mutual benefit to work within the system so both succeed and deliver information to the public, which in turn influences the direction of the government.

361. (D) The modern president is given far more responsibility than originally intended. The president has the daunting task of being responsible for government action and connecting with the American people so they trust him or her to do what is necessary. When the president is evasive, the news media that usually help deliver the message become a source of pressure to make sure that the administration is transparent in its operation.

362. **(B)** Personality plays a role in officials' interaction with the media, but everyone is eventually replaced, and the system continues to function. Reporters move to different areas of coverage or switch networks, and of course, elected officials leave office or are defeated, but the function of the interaction and often-reluctant cooperation remains the same.

363. **(C)** Public opinion is formed continuously, and the information people receive adds to that, but there is no deadline or time-sensitive aspect to what voters think. Granted, a breaking news story or emerging crisis may be important to them, but that information will be added to the aggregate public opinion that is constantly evolving.

364. **(B)** The link between media and government is information. Both sides need it, and both want it delivered in certain ways. The relationship that is created from this need is not always agreeable to both sides, but the connection will always remain.

365. **(D)** The media's main responsibility in delivering the news is to offer an explanation or clarity about what elected officials are doing and the effects legislation or policies may have.

366. **(D)** Facilitation is actually how the media impact the government. They deliver information about various players' actions and provide the public with a perspective on whether these actions are positive or negative.

367. **(C)** The judicial branch does not need public favor to survive as its members have lifelong tenure. This is not to say that the judiciary is deaf to public opinion or preference. However, the judiciary does not need to react to it as elected officials do. Also, the information that the news media receive from the judiciary is generally straightforward legal reasoning that may be debated by pundits but is mostly unambiguous.

368. **(B)** Linkage institutions are largely identified as political parties, campaigns, interest groups, and the media. This is largely how the public tends to interact with policy institutions such as Congress.

369. **(C)** By representing everyone over the age of 50, AARP is the largest interest group, but it is first and foremost a public interest group and also a brand that sells itself because its success is based on membership. The more members, the more money, which equals more political influence, which means more legislative success to recruit more members, and so on.

370. **(A)** This goes to the primary directive of elected officials to serve the public to ensure their personal success. The last thing any politician wants is the perception that he or she is in the pocket of "special interests" rather than fighting for constituents.

371. **(D)** All of the responses relate to the inverse relationship of public opinion and interest group influence. If opinion is high, the interest group's influence will be low. This may not seem correct, but if there is strong public opinion, politicians will react to that. Opposing views from interest groups will not receive much attention, and supporting views will not be needed.

PART 5   POLITICAL PARTICIPATION

Chapter 14: Parties in the American Political System

372. **(D)** Ticket splitting—voters' choice of one party at one level or branch of government and another party at a different level or branch of government—increased after the breakup of New Deal coalitions, because the allegiance to one party across the board was lost once the coalition fragmented and more factions arose seeking to further their own interests.

373. **(A)** House districts are much more local, while senators must meet the demands of an entire state. This obviously does not hold true for the eight states with only one congressional district. Typically the constituency for a senator will be much broader and cannot be broken down easily, so Senate candidates need to be more measured when campaigning, as they need to appeal to various political beliefs statewide.

374. **(C)** Party leaders want to make sure their party is unified and do not want to create a legislative or policy agenda that threatens that unity. Therefore, leaders concentrate on items with which all members agree as members of the party. For example, lower taxes for Republicans and better government services for Democrats.

375. **(D)** Elected officials want to be successful, and success is aided by their party being electorally successful. Thus, an individual member of the party does not want to drift too far from the collective center, because that may limit the ability to produce for his or her district. The collective action delivers specific goals that benefit all members of the party.

376. **(C)** If a political party has been successful in managing a crisis or handling the economy, its candidates will be rewarded at the polls, because in a campaign it is easier to point out what you have accomplished rather than what you plan to do.

377. **(D)** Voters tend to view parties favorably or unfavorably over time, and the parties' performance in elections reflects these views. These perceptions also help voters form opinions more quickly and easily, as they know basically where candidates stand and what they are likely to support.

378. **(A)** Political parties are designed to combine the efforts of like-minded individuals to promote a general ideology that will ensure local, state, and national success. This can only be accomplished through organization. If everyone ran alone, politics would remain regional, and it would be difficult for anyone to run for national office.

379. **(A)** Founders, such as James Madison, were concerned about factions disrupting the political process and causing disruptions within the system. The Constitution is designed to thwart the efforts of factions, which at the time might have created regional tyrannies through majority vote. Parties quickly developed over the main issue of a strong central government with authority. Parties formed and coalesced around the two titanic figures of Alexander Hamilton and Thomas Jefferson.

380. **(C)** Hamilton was the strongest, most intellectual proponent of the new Constitution and a strong central government, and he was the unquestioned leader of the Federalists in the early days of the republic.

381. (A) The organization of parties is continually focused on building coalitions to further their political aims. The better the organization, the better the coalitions, which in turn solidifies messaging and public perception with the goal of electoral victory through steadfast alliances.

382. (B) Messaging is important, and a cohesive party structure and organization facilitates messaging among all candidates. The more direct and unified the message, the easier it is for voters to understand where the candidates stand on issues.

383. (A) A party becomes successful by ensuring that it reaches the most potential voters possible and that those voters know where the party stands on issues. Additionally, parties need to know and act on the concerns of the public and public opinion on various issues. Polling is one way, but they must also try to find new ways to reach the electorate. Hence, every politician now has accounts on various social media networks.

384. (D) Each answer is necessary for party success, and the reasons were noted in earlier questions. Unifying messages and parameters within which candidates operate are vital for party identification and success.

385. (C) Proportional representation is used in most parliamentary systems around the world. This is not a winner-take-all system; rather representation is based on the proportion of the vote each party receives. This would undermine a two-party system, because third parties would receive some votes and would gain representation in the government.

386. (B) Because the structure of federalism is multiple governments over multiple levels, party unity can thrive. The local state representative caters to his or her constituents on local issues but also manages the party line on broader issues of national concern. For example, one Democrat in Billings, Montana, and another in Brooklyn, New York, have vastly different local needs but still form alliances on national issues like defense policy or gay marriage.

387. (A) Andrew Jackson was, in many ways, the first modern politician. He campaigned himself rather than letting others do it for him, and he sought to reach the American population at the grassroots level. To do this, party organization needed to be solidified nationally, not just regionally.

388. (D) Conventions were the next evolution in party politics. Conventions allied the local party leaders with national party leaders. The purpose was to choose a nominee for the presidential election, but conventions also secured the party's reach down to the local level of government.

389. (C) Patronage was the practice, initiated in large part by Andrew Jackson, of rewarding political supporters with government jobs. This was done by removing the political cronies of the previous administration, so government positions were often completely restaffed after every change in administration.

390. (A) Primaries, instituted through progressive reforms around the turn of the twentieth century, prevented party bosses from choosing the candidates that would appear on the ballot. By allowing voters to choose who would represent the party on the ticket, party bosses lost significant control of the party machines. No longer would a potential candidate have to kowtow to party bosses for a nomination. The Australian ballot, which made each vote anonymous, also reduced political bosses' power, but on a much more local level.

391. (B) Reforms that made elections more legitimate actually led to lower voter turnout, because the reforms—from registration laws to literacy tests (no longer allowed)—discouraged many from voting. This was especially true in lower-class and immigrant districts that were the foundation of party-boss power prior to the reforms.

392. (D) It may seem that parties also forge opinion through elections, but elections are the validation of parties and the tangible proof that all their work (referenced in the other answers) has paid off.

393. (A) Because they were no longer beholden to party bosses for their nominations, candidates could run on their own merits and appeal to voters directly to win primaries and then, hopefully, the general election.

394. (B) While the national convention is not the important nominating process it once was due to primaries, it still provides a large, visible venue of party unity and perspective.

395. (C) Progressive Era reforms sought to abolish the party machine system that ruled politics in the second half of the nineteenth century. Party bosses ruled through patronage, choosing what candidates would be running and making sure they knew who each voter chose at the ballot box.

396. (B) Parochialism means that local interests prevail. It is obvious why local concerns are important to members of Congress, as those are the concerns that will determine whether someone gets reelected.

397. (A) Parties are the easiest way for voters to identify where a candidate they may know little about stands on the issues. If a party is successful in an election, there is a strong chance that the individual candidate will be as well.

398. (B) Parties are able to collectively gather information and create platforms. Candidates follow these guidelines instead of having to outline all the issues separately.

399. (B) Political scientists at the time believed that parties were organized to assemble broad majorities to win elections. Therefore, parties promoted democracy because people were brought in rather than kept out of the political fold.

400. (C) At the time, many people believed that divided government caused gridlock. However, when Republicans took control of the House in 1994 with a Democratic president, legislation was still produced, and the country experienced tremendous economic growth.

401. (C) Legislation requires compromise. In a polarized system, compromise is more difficult to achieve because fewer members occupy the ideological center. That is not to say that nothing gets passed, but negotiating outcomes is more difficult because both sides are further apart.

402. (D) When a party wins, by a small or large margin, it has been put in power by the electorate. As such, the party is well served by assuming that it has a mandate to institute its agenda. Political reality usually sets in quickly; being the majority party in no way guarantees political success, but it does offer advantages for achieving success.

403. (B) The victorious party sets the policy agenda. The minority party forms an opposition to that agenda, and the two face off in creating legislation and establishing policy. This carries beyond Congress and touches the executive branch as well. Either the president has a majority in Congress, or it is divided government.

404. (C) The minority party in a polarized environment has little to gain by compromising. Perhaps it makes a few concessions, but it does not control the agenda or policy. Due to the polarization, the minority party may take a cynical approach and be obstructionist in the hope that the majority party will not be successful in implementing its policies and the electorate will remove it in the next election.

405. (C) At the founding of this country, there was already a need to push a policy agenda forward and draft legislation that was supportive of a political philosophy—in this instance, a strong central government over states' rights. The first parties formed to make sure that each side would get its way.

406. (A) The election of 1820 was toward the end of what was known as the Era of Good Feeling. America had won the War of 1812, and both North and South were without major conflict. The election was the reelection of James Monroe as president, and the Federalist Party had ceased to exist, leaving only one major party. This lack of political competition led the existing Democrats to disregard mobilization as they already held most offices. The lack of mobilization led to the dismal voter turnout.

407. (C) When the Republican Party formed in 1854, the Democratic Party was dominant; the other major party was the Whigs, which primarily represented northern business interests and was losing influence. With the passage of the Kansas-Nebraska Act, several smaller parties combined over the ideas of free soil and antislavery and quickly grew in the tumultuous political climate of the 1850s. Third parties may have an impact for an election or two, but only the Republicans permanently established themselves.

408. (B) Roosevelt's New Deal drastically increased the federal bureaucracy. The country, desperate for relief from the Great Depression, gave the Democrats and F.D.R. a true electoral mandate to alter the reach of the federal government through programs designed to help American citizens. This increase in spending and activity required many new government agencies that gave birth to the modern bureaucratic system.

409. (C) Today, the political climate and direction of policy is controlled by elected officials. Parties are important tools for organizing electoral success, and interest groups can also impact policy. However, ultimately, it is the action of those casting the votes for or against proposed legislation—or the president signing into law or issuing a veto—that determines government policy.

410. (B) America's winner-take-all system fosters the two-party structure because elections usually come down to one of two choices for most people. Taking into account Duverger's law, which holds that voters will jettison a third-party choice and vote for one of the two major candidates so their votes will count, it is little wonder that third parties have such a difficult time finding political traction.

411. (C) For policy initiatives to take hold, political parties have to package them in ways that appeal to the entire nation. Given the vast regional differences of the population, coordination is vital to secure support from the various regions.

412. (A) When one party dominates a political process, the threat of stagnation is possible. When debate is the best way to move forward between two parties, the public gets to hear both sides of an issue and decides at the polls. Neither party wants to lose political ground, so it is in their best interest to come to a compromise sometimes so they can both claim victory. The result is legislation and policy that may be stronger than that promoted by an unchallenged political force.

413. (A) There are benefits to compromising on the solution to a problem or issue. Typically, both sides have to give up something in order to get something, and the result, even in a polarized political environment, reflects the rational solution that benefits the most people and hurts the fewest.

414. (B) Rather than allowing regional issues to become national concerns, it is easier to tailor national policy and action to fit within different regions. In such a scenario, the elected official appears as the leading expert in the region and the person to be trusted to deliver for his or her constituents while serving in Washington.

415. (D) The budget, proposed by the president and passed by Congress, is the vehicle that party leaders use to influence policy. In the House, the Rules Committee sets the legislative agenda and can shape the budget. This committee is controlled by the majority party, so any part of the budget that does not agree with its political agenda will receive less attention than items that do. Thus, party leaders can influence policy.

Chapter 15: Campaigns, Elections, and Money

416. (D) It's been said that people vote with their pocket books. So voters tend to focus on economic issues in presidential election years. Good recent examples are George H.W. Bush's failed reelection bid when the economy went sour. In contrast, Bill Clinton was subjected to many scandals but was elected twice while enjoying a viberate economy.

417. (D) Voters go to the polls when they see activity for or against a candidate. Until recently, this was the focus of political parties and their mobilization efforts. The decline in these mobilization efforts has coincided with the decline in voter turnout.

418. (A) As noted earlier, the benefits of elections are collective; everyone reaps the reward even if they did not participate in the process. This is a classic "free-rider" problem inherent in representative democracy.

419. (B) While they may be distrustful of government, the elderly are the most active voting bloc because they are most affected by large government entitlements like Medicare and Social Security. There is no evidence that the elderly distrust the government; perhaps, to the contrary, they trust government more for the services they receive from it.

420. (D) Group differences appear in every politician's constituency and need to be factored into the positions that politician takes. To get elected or reelected, coalitions need to be built and the differences need to be understood.

421. (C) Out of these answers, only gun control is enough to motivate large groups of voters for or against it. Typically, it becomes of single-issue importance for those who believe their Second Amendment rights are being infringed by gun-control advocates rather than for those who would like to see greater restrictions on gun ownership. While some people may find the other issues important as well, there is no strong lobbying group for them as there is with gun control and the National Rifle Association (NRA).

422. (D) Competitive elections are the backbone of our federal republic and allow for all of these actions (and more) to occur. Public opinion and perspective provide the motivation for interest groups and politicians to mobilize to deliver what the American voter desires.

423. (D) The older and more educated you are, the more likely you are to pay attention to politics and be an active member of society through community or charity organizations or political campaigns. This means you are more likely to vote than are those who do not have as much education or are younger.

424. (B) Although relatively easy to do, voter registration has been identified as a roadblock to voting. Congress has recognized this and passed the Motor-Voter Act but studies have show the law has had little impact.

425. (C) Obviously, if incumbents remain with their political party because they fear losing if they leave the party, that is not going to be to their advantage. However, there have been candidates who have left their parties because of a difference of opinion and have been successful in reelection bids under their new party banner.

426. (D) Although few people claim to like negative campaigning, it continues to be used for its effectiveness in diminishing the standing of an opponent and remaining in voters' minds.

427. (B) All of these answers may seem to be legitimate, but although a candidate might like to track an opponent's expenditures, there is no ethical need for him or her to have that information. All other responses deal with either public funding or voter perception, which fall under the idea of campaigns being transparent.

428. **(C)** Because campaign financing is an important issue, FECA required full financial reporting by campaigns to ensure transparency and a level playing field of sorts. This law has been revised several times in the past 40 years to include the size of contributions.

429. **(A)** This case challenged FECA. The Supreme Court upheld most of the law's provisions but struck down spending limits as a First Amendment issue of free speech. The reasoning was that if the money was there to spend, why should a candidate not be allowed to get his or her message out?

430. **(C)** All of these responses are important. However, without money, all the other factors—from staff to name recognition—will not be possible and limit the person's chances for an electoral victory.

431. **(D)** The First Amendment, as it is currently interpreted by the Supreme Court, allows individuals to donate money to campaigns and causes that support campaigns as an expression of free speech. If one side is better at harnessing that money source, then the election will tip in favor of the better-funded candidate due to his or her ability to deliver messages through advertising and campaign events.

432. **(D)** Party labels provide voters with a good overview of where the candidate stands on issues. Parties have platforms that outline the positions they take, and while there may be some variation in beliefs from candidate to candidate, voters know the deviation is not going to be too significant or the candidate would not belong to that political party.

433. **(C)** Time after time, people surveyed believe in the institutions of government, just not the means by which those institutions continue to function. This disconnect is due in large part to the fact that few people have the time, energy, or inclination to follow the workings of government closely enough to witness how all the pieces come together.

434. **(A)** Voter apathy, or lack of caring, is a criticism leveled by leaders when faced with complaints from the electorate about candidate choice or government inaction. There may be some truth to the claim; however, it tends to be anecdotal at best, as there remains a strong contingent that actively participates in government and elections.

435. **(C)** The connection here is pretty straightforward—public opinion may lead to new candidates being elected, which will change the makeup of the legislature. This is true for all levels of government and is the basis for our electoral process.

436. **(D)** The candidate does not carry the party banner to win and therefore has to win based on individual performance. Public opinion and response to that opinion will influence votes and determine whether that candidate is elected. The control rests with the candidate based on what he or she demonstrates and the positions he or she takes.

437. **(A)** The desire to please the party takes precedence, as the party (not the candidate) determines success. Taking the party line, unlike in a candidate-centered environment, benefits those seeking electoral victory. Public opinion and voter response, while still important, are not quite as central a focus as are party considerations.

438. (B) Redistricting is a method used by the party in power to redraw districts in its favor. Obviously, moving district boundaries affects voter effectiveness.

439. (D) As party-centered politics transformed to candidate-centered politics during the 1950s and 1960s, spending increased because candidates created the message for themselves rather than following a message that the national party created. Thus, campaigns became more personal, not only in showcasing a candidate's qualifications, but also in attacking opponents.

440. (B) Through redistricting, parties in power have created districts that are political strongholds for incumbents. Many see this as undermining the democratic process, but parties' main focus is to continue to hold power, and redistricting enables them to do that more efficiently.

441. (D) Money is the foundation of a successful campaign. Campaigns are deemed successful if the candidate is victorious on election day, which only happens if voter turnout is higher for him or her than for opponents and if the candidate receives a positive public opinion.

442. (A) This does not mean that incumbents *are* unbeatable, but the electoral record shows that they have tremendous reelection success. This is due in large part to elected officials preventing legitimate challengers from entering the race who do not want to waste time and money on a losing campaign. If challenged, the incumbent may lose, but unless that is a strong possibility, most opponents will not begin a campaign.

443. (C) Voter opinion is key to electoral victory. If the voters approve of the job being done, it is highly unlikely that a challenger will step up to run against the incumbent.

444. (A) Due to its size (435 members), the House has uncontested elections every cycle. Candidates know if they have the backing of their constituents, and activists keep abreast of electoral politics to determine vulnerability. This ability to anticipate helps determine whether a challenger for the seat has a chance.

445. (B) The electorate may see anticipation as arrogance, and the candidate may suffer because voters do not like to feel that their decisions are so predictable. Even though this may be counterproductive if the candidate has served the district well, an organized opponent may be able to take advantage if he or she feels an official's standing slipping.

446. (D) Voters need to know what candidates stand for. This is true even for incumbents who may have held their seats for some time. If there is a mixed or unclear message, voters will begin to look elsewhere for their choices.

447. (A) Few people admit that they like or appreciate negative campaigning, but it does appear to be effective and will therefore continue to be used. Promoting doubt about a candidate by revealing a personal scandal or questionable votes is a way to dismantle any trust he or she may have built up with voters.

448. (B) Obviously the person with the most votes wins, but the strategy behind campaigns is to energize your voter base while demoralizing the base of your opponent. A candidate can overwhelm an opponent through a successful display of poise, experience, and leadership. However, the qualifications of candidates for higher offices (such as governor, senator, or president) are rarely far apart; therefore, negative campaigning is used to manufacture differences to keep the other side's voters at home.

449. (C) Senators McCain and Feingold—Republican and Democrat, respectively—joined forces to create legislation that ended "soft money," money donated in unrestricted sums to political parties, which then distributed it to campaigns with little or no oversight.

450. (A) Term limits appeal to many, but a significant drawback is the inability to hold elected officials accountable over time. If an official knows that his or her time in office is ending, there is no impetus for that official to act out of anything except self-interest. Officials disregard party and electoral politics, and critics argue that voters suffer because politicians disregard their constituents' needs as their tenures draw to a close.

451. (B) A presidential election is by far the most important, as it is the only national election. Politically, the landscape changes when a new president comes into office; therefore, new policy initiatives will be put into effect.

452. (C) Throughout this nation's history, there have been elections that have changed, not only the party in power, but the alliances of each party. Abraham Lincoln, Franklin D. Roosevelt, and Ronald Reagan are all presidents who won elections and turned the tide of electoral politics for at least a generation afterward.

453. (B) An authorizing election is an election that may not have the seismic political power of a realignment election but is significant in that the electorate has agreed to give challengers a chance to prove themselves. The congressional election of 1994, when the Republicans took control of the House for the first time in 40 years, is a prime example of an authorizing election.

454. (A) Focus groups are a marketing tool in which average citizens are observed discussing a product. In a political scenario, the group may discuss certain policies or participants' perceptions of a politician. This information is vital to pollsters, political staffers, and politicians in determining what political course to take.

455. (D) Those winning elections have been chosen for their stances on issues and what direction they plan to take on public policy concerns. The results of an election demonstrate how politicians should coordinate their agendas moving forward.

Chapter 16: The Media, Interest Groups and the American Public

456. (C) Gridlock occurs because interest groups compete with each other over two sides of the same issue. One wins politicians to its side, while the other wins politicians as well, and no policy is furthered.

457. (A) For a policy to be enacted, elected officials have to pass legislation. It makes sense for interest groups to cultivate relationships with these officials.

458. (D) Interest groups appeal to politicians through lobbying. Recently this practice has come under closer public scrutiny because of the misdeeds of a few who offered gifts and bribes for support of their agendas. But overall, lobbyists serve an important function to elected officials, as they provide information and feedback on the public's view of issues.

459. (B) Fearing factions and the overriding of duly elected officials, James Madison and Alexis de Tocqueville viewed interest groups as corrupting the process of government by setting narrow agendas that appealed to only a few instead of the many. The people would not be heard over the more organized and vocal minority of interest groups spurring government action.

460. (D) Both A and B are correct because interest groups count on the fact that officials need them as much as they need officials. Further, there is more than one way to get the attention of government, and if one way fails, interest groups try to move their agendas through other avenues—for example, if Congress is unresponsive, perhaps the president will take action.

461. (A) The organizational resources of most interest groups, from policy experts to lawyers, enable these groups to have more access to politicians and make connections with elected officials.

462. (D) Small special interest groups may focus on an issue that does not reach most voters, and even if it does reach them, they are disinterested. For example, milk subsidies to dairy farmers are not of pressing national concern. However, it is vital to those farmers and their lobby, so they are quite vocal about it. Politicians listening to issues and not hearing any counterpoint from voters will support the small lobby's initiatives.

463. (A) Citizens become involved in certain groups because they believe it is the right thing to do. They agree with the agenda but participate because the issue is one for which they feel there is a clear right and wrong. The environment is an example of this kind of issue.

464. (A) The free-rider problem is often associated with interest groups, as people may be for the cause but do little to further it. Denial of benefits is a way to make sure that members participate.

465. (C) Interest groups, a major linkage institution in our political system, operate all throughout the United States but the major players have their offices on K Street in Washington, D.C. This makes the street a major power hub in the capitol.

466. (A) When an interest group is out of power with those in control of the government, it is easier to excite the base and gain new membership by playing the part of the underdog or outsider to the existing system.

467. (A) The better the technology, the easier it is to connect. Witness the political importance of social networks in the political process. The more support an interest group has, the more politically powerful it becomes.

468. (B) Occasionally, politicians will seek to garner greater support by suggesting the formation of an interest group around an issue that affects part of the population. The federal system of multiple-level governance creates an environment in which an interest group's activities can be on different levels and the supporting politicians benefit.

469. (A) Knowledge is power, and interest groups seek to educate politicians. More important, they seek to educate the public that is affected by the issue. Without public support, an interest group's political power evaporates.

470. (D) The larger the issue, the more difficult it is to address through one organization. Just as Congress creates committees to address legislative issues, interest groups must sometimes splinter to address the different concerns that fall under a larger issue. For example, a group dedicated to eradicating cancer can be linked with groups focused on ending specific types of cancer.

471. (D) Professional is not a category for PACs. There are PACs for all of the other categories listed. Some may cooperate with each other to gain political advantage.

472. (B) Congressional committees are the pivotal point at which legislation either moves forward or fails. By influencing committee activity, PACs can move relatively narrow issues that don't appeal or affect most of the public forward on the committee agenda.

473. (C) This obviously pertains to PACs that do not have an inside track to politicians in control. They therefore spend their energy trying to change the political landscape.

474. (D) Money is the most important thing for political campaigns, and because PACs spend large amounts on issues to make the public aware, elected officials would be foolish to ignore them.

475. (A) Although PACs receive a lot of attention regarding campaign financing, they make up a small percentage of interest group activity. Their activities are not up to voter approval or rejection, so voter action is no barrier to what they do.

476. (A) Scorekeeper is one of the three major roles the media plays in American politics. In this role the media is interested in "who is winning" and largely devoid of substance. The media has been under attack for making this role too important and deviating away from campaign issues.

477. (C) In the role of gatekeeper the media determines what is newsworthy and what is not. Critics contend that the media becomes an agenda setter with their own motives instead of an information giver and truth seeker.

478. (C) Lobbyists are able to shape opinion and policy because they have the numbers to get noticed by elected officials.

479. (D) As noted earlier, the complexity and volume of business to be done necessitated the creation of lobbyists. As the government grew, so did the number of lobbyists.

480. **(A)** As in anything, competition can be detrimental to the well-being of an organization if that competitor is able to do the same thing just as effectively. Interest groups with the same focus may cannibalize support for their cause, because they are competing for the same members and their political voice is lost.

481. **(D)** This speaks to the expertise that interest groups provide. Political information explains how the public feels, but the technical information helps elected officials decide whether action is politically worth the risk of association.

482. **(B)** The *Register* comprises tens of thousands of pages of all the bureaucratic rules, regulations, and procedures for every government agency in existence. Although massive, it is an invaluable resource for the acceptable actions of government bureaucracy.

483. **(C)** Public demonstrations and protests, symbolized in the efforts of the youth of the 1960s on behalf of causes from civil rights to Vietnam, provide interest groups with a powerful political voice because they are extremely visible. Politicians are often forced to react in a way that clearly shows their positions in the debate.

484. **(A)** The foundation of many successful lobbying campaigns, grassroots lobbying requires an organization to contact large portions of the public. As membership grows, so does the political force of the organization.

485. **(D)** Through grassroots, it may appear that constituents are reaching out to their politicians to affect change, which is true. This has a much more significant effect, as politicians are not talking to Washington lobbyists but to residents of their congressional districts. As previously noted, elected officials' main goal is to get reelected, so they will be much more responsive to their constituents' views on an issue.

486. **(B)** Although covered greatly by the news media and public commentators, PACs contribute a relatively small part to political movements and campaigns compared to direct donations.

487. **(C)** Although it is often a contentious relationship, government officials and the media need each other to succeed. The former provides the information the latter needs, and the latter delivers it to the public, which the former requires.

488. **(A)** Government must be responsive to the people. The modern media have forced Congress and presidents to be more transparent in their activities. No longer is business conducted mostly behind closed doors. Everything is in the open, and the public knows where politicians stand and what actions they have taken. This increased accountability has given the media a great responsibility to continue to deliver the news in an unbiased, straightforward way so the public can make informed decisions.

489. **(B)** This is an extension of the previous question. The media assess legislation and activity, and elected officials respond to those assessments. The influence is powerful, but not because the media tell legislators how to vote; rather, the public takes action due to the media coverage and the influence the media have on public opinion.

490. (A) News coverage is not entirely based on what the government is doing. More often than not, the media cover other pressing social concerns. Through this coverage, they inform politicians about issues that the politicians may be interested in addressing to meet the needs and concerns of their constituents.

491. (B) News organizations have combined to conduct public opinion polls. These polls take the public temperature on issues important to the public. This offers a service to most elected officials who cannot conduct their own polls as frequently due to a lack of resources. The president has internal pollsters, but the average House member does not.

492. (C) Information is key to the success of interest groups and politicians, which is why both cultivate relationships with the media. This is to make sure that their messages get out to the public and that the public's concerns reach them as soon as possible so they can appear to address such concerns quickly. In politics, the image of taking quick and decisive action is vital to continued success.

493. (D) The press delivers the news, and public policy activities are news. The public is made aware of what is going on, and the policy continues to change with the needs and desires of the public.

494. (D) The responses to this question are straightforward. Provide elected officials with a popular benefit that appeals to everyone nationwide, and you will have a successful lobbying effort.

495. (D) Interest groups are interested in pushing policy forward, but once legislation leaves committee, it is debated by all members. If interest groups concentrated only on committee members, they would not have any influence once Congress as a whole debated the issue. All other responses here are limitations, but interest groups are best served by contacting as many members of Congress as possible.

496. (A) Elected officials rely on the expertise interest groups provide on a given issue. The groups have an agenda; this is no secret to officials, but the expertise is important and provides them with a much-needed resource.

497. (B) Cost-benefit analysis is the only true way of determining the focus of an initiative. This does not necessarily mean seeing how much the initiative will actually cost, although expenditures are important. It can also be an analysis done by a politician to see whether any political cost will be outweighed by the political benefit. If it is worth it, the policy is supported; otherwise, it is not.

498. (B) Loopholes are meant to provide tax avoidance for certain interests. This might solidify political support, but it runs counter to the business of government to collect revenue to provide services. Everyone would like services without having to pay for them. Individuals do not have the opportunity to negotiate such allowances, but an interest group with political power can do so for the industry it represents.

499. (D) Interest groups that can successfully frame an issue as something that will affect an elected official's constituents are guaranteed to be heard. If the argument is successful, the group will most likely gain the political support it seeks.

500. (B) When an issue is discussed more in public opinion, interest groups have less influence. This is not to say their influence disappears, but if the public is aware of the issue and is generally decided, interest groups for the opposing view will not have much political clout. Interest groups pursuing the same view as that favored by the public will have less influence as well because elected officials will base their decisions on the known public opinion.

BIBLIOGRAPHY

Aberbach, Joel D., and Mark A. Peterson. *The Executive Branch*. New York: Oxford University Press, 2005.

Cayton, Andrew R. L. *America: Pathways to the Present*. Boston, MA: Pearson/Prentice Hall, 2007.

Danzer, Gerald A., J. Jorge Klor De Alva, and Larry S. Krieger. *The Americans: A History*. Evanston, IL: McDougal Littell/Houghton Mifflin, 2006.

Epstein, Lee, and Thomas G. Walker. *Institutional Powers and Constraints*. Washington, DC: CQ Press, 2011.

Gunther, Gerald. *Constitutional Law*. 12th ed. Westbury, NY: The Foundation Press, Inc., 1991.

Hall, Kermit L., and Kevin T. McGuire. *The Judicial Branch*. New York: Oxford University Press, 2005.

Kennedy, David M., Lizabeth Cohen, and Thomas Andrew Bailey. *The American Pageant: A History of the Republic*. Boston, MA: Houghton Mifflin, 2006.

Kernell, Samuel, Gary C. Jacobson, and Thad Kousser. *The Logic of American Politics*. Washington, DC: CQ Press, 2009.

Mayhew, David R. *Parties and Politics: How the American Government Works*. New Haven: Yale University Press, 2008.

Overholser, Geneva, and Kathleen Hall Jamieson. *The Press*. New York: Oxford University Press, 2005.

Quirk, Paul J., and Sarah A. Binder. *The Legislative Branch*. New York: Oxford University Press, 2005.